Post-capitalist Society

Other books by Peter F. Drucker

Management

Managing for the Future
Managing the Non-profit Organization
The Frontiers of Management
Innovation and Entrepreneurship
Management: Tasks, Responsibilities, Practices
The Effective Executive
Managing for Results
The Practice of Management
The Changing World of the Executive
Managing in Turbulent Times
The New Markets and Other Essays
Concept of the Corporation

Economics, politics, society

The New Realities
Toward the Next Economics
The Unseen Revolution
Men, Ideas and Politics
The Age of Discontinuity
The Landmarks of Tomorrow
America's Next Twenty Years
The New Society
The Future of Industrial Man
The End of Economic Man

Fiction

The Temptation to Do Good
The Last of All Possible Worlds

Autobiography

Adventures of a Bystander

Post-capitalist Society

Peter F. Drucker

UTTERWORTH
EINEMANN

Butterworth-Heinemann Ltd
Linacre House, Jordan Hill, Oxford OX2 8DP

⟨R A member of the Reed Elsevier group

OXFORD LONDON BOSTON
MUNICH NEW DELHI SINGAPORE SYDNEY
TOKYO TORONTO WELLINGTON

First published 1993
Reprinted 1993

British Library Cataloguing in Publication Data
Drucker, Peter F.
   Post-capitalist Society
   I. Title
   330.12

ISBN 0 7506 0921 4

Set by Hope Services (Abingdon) Ltd
Printed in England by Clays Ltd, St Ives plc

Contents

Acknowledgements

This book owes much to my long-time US editor and friend Cass Canfield, Jr. He patiently endured countless proposals and outlines and encouraged me at every step. He carefully read my manuscripts and made most helpful suggestions and criticisms. Thanks are due also to another long-time friend, Marion Buhagiar, who read and reviewed the book's first completed draft and helped greatly in revising and editing it. The biographer of Frederick Winslow Taylor, Professor Ronald Greenwood of GMI, the General Motors Engineering and Management Institute in Flint, Michigan, critically read my comments on Taylor and Scientific Management (in Chapter 1). The last section of Chapter 6 owes a debt to the late Robert Greenleaf (especially to his wise little book, *Servant Leadership* (Paulist Press, 1977) and to *Leadership as an Art* by Max de Pree, (Doubleday, 1990), and to a good many discussions with these two friends and with Dr David Allan Hubbard, the President of Fuller Theological Seminary in Pasadena, California. My assistant Holly Hauck over a long year bravely coped with the vagaries of my handwriting. To all of them my warmest thanks.

Claremont, California
Thanksgiving Day 1992

Introduction: the transformation

Every few hundred years in Western history there occurs a sharp *transformation*. We cross what in an earlier book (*The New Realities*, 1989) I called a 'divide'. Within a few short decades, society rearranges itself – its world view; its basic values; its social and political structure; its arts; its key institutions. Fifty years later there is a new world. And the people born then cannot even imagine the world in which their grandparents lived and into which their own parents were born.

We are currently living in such a transformation. It is creating the Post-capitalist society. This is the subject of this book.

One such transformation occurred in the thirteenth century – when the European world, almost overnight, became centred in the new city – with the emergence of city guilds as the new dominant social groups and with the revival of long-distance trade; with the Gothic, that eminently urban, indeed practically bourgeois, new architecture; with the new painting of the Sienese; with the shift to Aristotle as the fountainhead of wisdom; with urban universities replacing as the centres of culture the monasteries in their rural isolation; with the new urban Orders, the Dominicans and Franciscans, emerging – as the carriers of religion, of learning, of spirituality; and within a few decades, with the shift from Latin to the vernacular and with Dante creating *European* literature.

Two hundred years later, the next transformation took place in the 60 years between Gutenberg's invention in 1455 of printing with movable type, and with it of the printed book, and Luther's Protestant Reformation in 1517. These were the decades of the blossoming of the Renaissance, peaking between 1470 and 1500 in Florence and Venice; of the rediscovery of Antiquity; of the European discovery of America; of the Spanish Infantry, the first standing army since the Roman Legions; of the rediscovery of anatomy and with it of scientific inquiry; and of the general adoption of Arabic numerals in the West. And again, no one living in 1520 could have imagined the world in which one's grandparents had lived and into which one's parents had been born.

The next transformation began in 1776 – the year of the American Revolution, of Watt's perfected steam engine and of Adam Smith's *Wealth of Nations*. It came to a conclusion 40 years later, at Waterloo – 40 years during which all modern 'isms' were born. Capitalism, Communism and the Industrial Revolution emerged during these decades. These years saw also the creation – in 1809 – of the modern university (Berlin) but also of universal schooling. These four decades brought the Emancipation of the Jews – and by 1815 the Rothschilds had become the Great Power overshadowing kings and princes. These 40 years produced, in effect, a new European civilization. Again, no one living in 1820 could imagine the world in which one's grandparents had lived and into which one's parents had been born.

Our time, 200 years later, is again such a period of transformation. This time it is not, however, confined to Western society and Western history. It is one of the fundamental changes that there is no longer a 'Western' history or indeed a 'Western' civilization. There is only world history and world civilization – but both are 'Westernized'. It is moot whether this present transformation began with the emergence of the first non-Western country, Japan, as a Great Economic Power – that is, around 1960 – or with the computer, that is, with information becoming central. My own candidate would be the American GI Bill of Rights after World War II which gave every returning American soldier the money to attend a university – something that would have made absolutely no sense only 30 years earlier, at the end of World War I. The GI Bill of Rights – and the enthusiastic response to it on the part of America's veterans – signalled the shift to the knowledge society. Future historians may well consider it the most important event of the twentieth century.

We are clearly still in the middle of this transformation – indeed, if history is any guide it will not be completed until 2010 or 2020. But it has already changed the political, economic, social and moral landscape of the world. No one born in 1990 could possibly imagine the world in which one's grandparents (i.e. my generation) had grown up and in which one's own parents had been born.

The first successful attempt to understand the transformation that turned the Middle Ages and the Renaissance into the Modern World, the transformation that began in 1455, was not even attempted until 50 years later: with the *Commentaries* of Copernicus, written between 1510 and 1514; with Machiavelli's *Prince*, written in 1513; with Michelangelo's synthesis and transcendence of all Renaissance art in the ceiling of the Sistine Chapel painted between 1510 and 1512; and with the re-establishment of the Catholic Church at the Tridentine Council in the 1530s.

The next transformation – the one that occurred 200 years ago and was ushered in by the American Revolution – was first understood and analysed 60 years later, in the two volumes of Alexis de Tocqueville's *Democracy in America*, published, respectively, in 1835 and 1840.

We are far enough advanced into the new post-capitalist society to review and revise the social, economic and political history of the Age of Capitalism and of the nation state. This book will therefore take new looks at the period we are leaving behind – and some of the things it sees from its new vantage point may come as distinct surprises (they did to me).

To foresee what the post-capitalist world itself will look like is, however, risky still. What new questions will arise and where the big new issues will lie, we can, I believe, already discover with some degree of probability. In many areas we can also describe what will *not* work. 'Answers' to most questions are still largely hidden in the womb of the future. The one thing we can be sure of is that the world that will emerge from the present rearrangement of values, of beliefs, of social and economic structures, of political concepts and systems, indeed of world views, will be different from anything anyone today imagines. In some areas – and especially in society and its structure – basic shifts have, however, already happened. That the new society will be both a non-socialist and a post-capitalist society is practically certain. And it is certain also that its primary resource will be knowledge. This also means that it will have to be a society of organizations. Certain it is also that in politics we have already shifted from the 400 years of the sovereign nation state to a pluralism in which the nation state will be one rather than the only unit of political integration. It will be one component – though still a key component – in what I call the 'post-capitalist polity', a system in which transnational, regional, nation-state and local, indeed tribal, structures compete and co-exist.

These things have already happened. They can therefore be described. To do this is the purpose of this book.

Post-capitalist society and post-capitalist polity

Only a few short decades ago everybody 'knew' that a post-capitalist society would surely be a Marxist one. Now we all know that a Marxist society is the one thing the next society is not going to be. But most of us also know – or at least sense – that developed countries are moving out of anything that could be called capitalism. The market will surely remain the effective integrator of *economic* activity. But as a *society* the developed countries have also already moved into post-capitalism. It is fast becoming a society of new 'classes' and with a new central resource as its core.

Capitalist society was dominated by two social classes: the capitalists, who owned and controlled the means of production, and the workers – Karl Marx's (1818-1883) 'proletarians', alienated, exploited, dependent. The proletarians first became the 'affluent' middle class as a result of the 'Productivity Revolution' – the revolution that began at the very time of Marx's death in 1883, and reached its climax in every developed country shortly after World War II. Around 1950 the industrial worker – no longer a 'proletarian' but still 'labour' – seemed to dominate politics and society in every developed country. But then, with the onset of the 'Management Revolution' the blue-collar workers in manufacturing industry rapidly began to decline both in numbers and even more in power and status. By the year 2000 there will be no developed country where traditional workers making and moving goods account for more than one-sixth or one-eighth of the workforce.

The capitalist probably reached his peak even earlier – by the turn of the century, and surely no later than World War I. Since then no one has matched in power and visibility the likes of

Morgan, Rockefeller, Carnegie or Ford in the United States; Siemens, Thysen, Rathenau, Krupp in Germany; Mond, Cunard, Lever, Vickers, Armstrong in England; de Wendel and Schneider in France; or of the families that owned the great *zaibatsu* of Japan; Mitsubishi, Mitsui and Sumitomo. By World War II they had all been replaced by 'professional managers'* – the first result of the Management Revolution. There are still a great many rich people around, of course, and they are still prominent in the newspapers' society pages. But they have become 'celebrities'; economically they have almost ceased to matter. Even on the business pages all attention is being paid to 'hired hands', that is, to managers. And such talk of money as there is, is about the 'excessive salaries' and bonuses of such hired hands who themselves own little or nothing.

Instead of the old-line capitalist, in developed countries pension funds increasingly control the supply and allocation of money. In the United States they owned in 1992 half of the share capital of the country's large businesses and held almost as much of these companies' fixed debts. The beneficiary owners of the pension funds are, of course, the country's employees. If Socialism is defined, as Marx defined it, as ownership of the means of production by the employees, then the United States has become the most 'socialist' country around – while still being the most 'capitalist' one as well. Pension funds are run by a new breed of capitalists, the faceless, anonymous, salaried employees, the pension funds' investment analysts and portfolio managers.

But equally important: the real and controlling resource and the absolutely decisive 'factor of production' is now neither capital, nor land, nor labour. It is knowledge. Instead of capitalists and proletarians, the classes of the post-capitalist society are knowledge workers and service workers.

The shift to the knowledge society

The move to the post-capitalist society began shortly after World War II. I first wrote of the 'employee society' even before 1950.† Ten years later, around 1960, I coined the terms 'knowledge work'

---

* The best account, though limited to manufacturing in the United States, is Alfred D. Chandler's book *The Visible Hand* (Harvard University Press, 1977).

† e.g. in my book *The New Society* (1949).

and 'knowledge worker'. And my 1969 book *The Age of Discontinuity* first talked of the 'society of organizations'. This book is thus based on work done over 40 years. And most of its policy and action recommendations have been successfully tested.

Only with the collapse of Marxism as an ideology and of Communism as a system* did it, however, become completely clear that we have already moved into a new and different society. Only then did a book like this become possible: a book that is not prediction but description, a book that is not *futuristic* but calls for action here and now.

The bankruptcy – moral, political, economic – of Marxism and the collapse of the Communist regimes were not 'The End of History' (as a widely publicized 1989 article† proclaimed). Even the staunchest believers in the free market surely hesitate to hail its triumph as the Second Coming. But the events of 1989 and 1990 were more than just the end of an era; they signified the end of *one kind of history*. The collapse of Marxism and of Communism brought to a close 250 years that were dominated by a secular religion – I have called it‡ the *belief in salvation by society*. The first prophet of this secular religion was Jean-Jacques Rousseau (1712–1778). The Marxist Utopia was its ultimate distillation – and its apotheosis.

The same forces which destroyed Marxism as an ideology and Communism as a social system, are, however, also making capitalism obsolescent. For 250 years, from the second half of the eighteenth century on, capitalism was the dominant social reality. For the last hundred years Marxism was the dominant social ideology. Both are rapidly being superseded by a new and very different society.

The new society – and it is already here – is a post-capitalist society. It surely, to say it again, will use the free market as the one proven mechanism of economic integration. It will not be an 'anticapitalist society'. It will not even be a 'non-capitalist society'; the institutions of capitalism will survive though some, e.g. banks, may play quite different roles. But the centre of gravity in the post-capitalist society – its structure; its social and economic

---

* Both anticipated in a book of mine *The New Realities* – published in 1989 and written in 1987, several years ahead of the actual events.

† 'The End of History' by Francis Fukayama, *The National Interest*, Summer 1989.

‡ in my book *The New Realities* (1989).

dynamics; its social classes and its social problems – are different from those that dominated the last 250 years, and defined the issues around which political parties, social groups, social value systems, and personal and political commitments crystallized.

The basic economic resource – 'the means of production' to use the economist's term – is no longer capital, nor natural resources (the economist's 'land'), nor 'labour'. *It is and will be knowledge.* The central wealth-creating activities will be neither the allocation of capital to productive uses nor 'labour' – the two poles of nineteenth- and twentieth-century economic theory, whether Classical, Marxist, Keynesian or Neo-Classical. Value is now created by 'productivity' and 'innovation', both applications of knowledge to work. The leading social groups of the knowledge society will be 'knowledge workers' – knowledge executives who know how to allocate knowledge to productive use – just as the capitalists knew how to allocate capital to productive use; knowledge professionals; knowledge employees. Practically all these knowledge people will be employed in organizations. Yet unlike the employees under capitalism they own both the 'means of production' and the 'tools of production' – the former through their pension funds which are rapidly emerging in all developed countries as the only real owners, the latter because knowledge workers own their knowledge and can take it with them wherever they go. The *economic* challenge of the post-capitalist society will therefore be the productivity of knowledge work and knowledge worker.

The *social* challenge of the post-capitalist society will, however, be the dignity of the second class in post-capitalist society: the service workers. Service workers, as a rule, lack the necessary education to be knowledge workers. And in every country, even the most highly advanced ones, they will constitute a majority.

The post-capitalist society will be divided by a new dichotomy of values and of aesthetic perceptions. It will not be the 'Two Cultures' – the literary culture and the scientific culture – of which the English novelist, scientist, and government administrator C. P. Snow (1905–1980) wrote in his 1959 book *The Two Cultures and the Scientific Revolution* – though that split is real enough. The dichotomy will be between 'intellectuals' and 'managers', the former concerned with words and ideas, the latter with people and work. To transcend this dichotomy in a new synthesis will be a central philosophical and educational challenge for the post-capitalist society.

Outflanking the nation state?

The late 1980s and early 1990s also marked the end of another era, another 'kind of history'. If the fall of the Berlin Wall in 1989 was the climactic event that symbolized the fall of Marxism and Communism, the transnational coalition against Iraq's invasion of Kuwait in February 1991 was the climactic event that marked the end of the 400 years of history in which the *sovereign nation state* was the main (and often the only) actor on the political stage. Future historians will surely rank February 1991 among the 'big dates'. There is no precedent for such transnational actions. At no earlier occasion did nations – without a single dissenter of conse-quence (and almost without dissent altogether) – put the common interest of the world community in putting down terrorism ahead of their own national sentiments, and, in many cases, ahead even of their own national interest. There is no precedent for the all but universal realization that terrorism is not a matter of 'politics' to be left to individual national governments. It requires non-national, transnational action.

It is widely believed, especially among Liberals in the United States, that the 1991 war against Iraq was mounted to protect the West's oil supply. Nothing could be further from the truth. Iraqi control of the oil wells of Kuwait – and those of Saudi Arabia as well – would have been very much in the West's *economic* interest. It would have meant *much cheaper oil*. For while Kuwait and Saudi Arabia have practically no native populations and therefore no urgent need for immediate petroleum income, Iraq is heavily overpopulated, and, except for petroleum, almost totally without natural resources. It therefore needs to sell as much oil as it possi-bly can whereas Kuwait and Saudi Arabia are primarily inter-ested in keeping oil prices high and that means keeping production low. This, by the way, explains why the United States heavily supported Saddam Hussein's regime in Iraq, even before the Iraq-Iran war and why it continued to do so until the very moment when Saddam attacked Kuwait and thus indulged in an overt terrorist act. It also explains, I suspect, why Saddam miscal-culated; he must have been convinced that the United States would let him get away with flagrant aggression in order to ensure *low* petroleum prices. And everyone I know in a major petroleum company was sure when Iraq invaded Kuwait that the

US government would not do anything but make a few disapproving noises.

In the 400 years since the French lawyer-politician Jean Bodin (1530–1596) invented it (in his 1576 book *Six Livres de la Republique*) the *nation state* had become the one organ of political power, internally and externally. And since the French Revolution, i.e. in the last 200 years, it also became the carrier of the secular religion, the belief in salvation by society. In fact Totalitarianism – Communist as well as Nazi – was the ultimate distillation and apotheosis of the doctrine of the sovereign nation state as the one and only organ of power.

Political theory and constitutional law still know only the sovereign state. And in the last hundred years it has steadily become more powerful and more dominant. It has mutated into the 'Megastate'. It is the one political structure we so far understand, are familiar with, and know how to build out of prefabricated and standardized parts, an executive, a legislature, courts, a diplomatic service, national armies, and so on. Every one of the nearly 200 new countries that have been carved out of the former colonial empires since the end of World War II has been set up as a sovereign nation state. And this is what every one of the various parts of the last of the colonial empires, the Soviet empire, aspires to become.

And yet for 40 years, that is, since the end of World War II, the sovereign nation state has steadily been losing its position as the *one* organ of power. Internally, developed countries are fast becoming pluralist societies of organizations. Externally, some governmental functions are becoming transnational, others regional (i.e. in the European Community), others are being tribalized.

The nation state is not going to 'wither away'. It may remain the most powerful political organ around for a long time to come. But it will no longer be the indispensable one. It will increasingly share power with other organs, other institutions, other policy makers. What is to remain the domain of the nation state? What is to be carried out within the state by autonomous institutions? What is to be 'supernational'? What is to be 'transnational'? What is to be 'separate and local'? These questions will be central political issues for decades to come. In its specifics, the outcome is quite unpredictable. But the political order will look different from the political order of the last centuries in which the players differed in size, wealth, constitutional arrangements and political creed but were uniform as nation states, each sovereign within its territory, and each defined by its territory. We are moving – we have indeed already moved – into *post-capitalist polity*.

The last of what might be called the 'pre-modern' philosophers, Gottfried Leibnitz (1646–1716), spent much of his life in a futile attempt to restore the unity of Christendom. His motivation was not the fear of religious wars between Catholics and Protestants or between different Protestant sects – that danger was already past when Leibnitz was born. He feared that without a common belief in a supernatural God, secular religions would emerge. And a secular religion, he was convinced would, almost by definition, have to be a tyranny and suppress the freedom of the person.

A century later Jean-Jacques Rousseau confirmed Leibnitz's fears. Rousseau asserted that *society* could and should control the individual human being. It could and should create a 'New Adam'. It could and should create universal human perfection. But it also could and should subordinate the individual to the impersonal, super-personal *volonté génerale* (the general will) – what Marxists later came to call the 'objective laws of history'. Since the French Revolution Salvation by Society gradually became the dominant creed at first in the West, and since World War II worldwide. However much it pretends to be 'anti-religious', it is a religious faith. The means are, of course, non-spiritual: banning alcohol; killing all Jews; universal psychoanalysis; abolition of private property. The goal, however, is religious: establishing the Kingdom of God on Earth through creating the 'New Man'.

For more than a hundred years the most powerful and the most pervasive secular creed promising salvation through society was Marxism. The religious promise of Marxism far more than its convoluted ideology and its increasingly unrealistic economics constituted its tremendous appeal, especially to intellectuals. There were many reasons, for instance, for Eastern Jews to accept an ideology that promised an end to their persecution and their discrimination in the Russia of the Tsars or in Romania. But the most powerful appeal for them was Marxism's promise of an earthly paradise, that is, Marxism's appeal as a secular religion.

Communism collapsed as an economic system. Instead of creating wealth it created misery. Instead of creating economic quality it created a *nomenklatura* of functionaries enjoying unprecedented economic privileges. But as a *creed*, Marxism collapsed because it did not create the 'New Man'. Instead it brought out and strengthened all the worst in the 'Old Adam': corruption, greed and lust for power; envy and mutual distrust; petty tyranny and secretiveness; lying, stealing, denunciation and, above all, cynicism. Communism, the system, had its heroes. But Marxism, the creed, did not have a single saint.

The human being may well be beyond redemption. The Latin poet may have been right: human nature always sneaks in through the back door no matter how many times the pitchfork tosses it out the front door. Maybe the cynics are right who assert that there is no virtue, no goodness, no selflessness, only self-interest and hypocrisy (though there are enough witnesses to the contrary, as I remind myself in my darkest hours).

But surely the collapse of Marxism as a creed signifies the end of the belief in Salvation by Society. What will emerge we cannot know – we can only hope and pray. Perhaps nothing beyond stoic resignation? Perhaps a rebirth of traditional religion addressing itself to the needs and challenges of the person in the knowledge society? The explosive growth of what I call 'pastoral' Christian churches in America – Protestant, Catholic, Non-Denominational – might be a portent. But so might be the resurgence of Fundamentalist Islam. For the young people in the Moslem world who now so fervently embrace Islamic Fundamentalism would, 40 years ago, have been equally fervent Marxists. Or will there be new religions?

What is unlikely to happen is easier to forecast than what is likely to happen. We will not see the rejection of material values and of technology – the 'Return to the Middle Ages' – which a Japanese writer, Taichi Sakaya (born 1935), predicted in a Japanese best-seller of the mid-1980s (published in English in 1991 by Kodansha International, New York–Tokyo–London, under the title *The Knowledge-Value Revolution*). The worldwide spread of information and of technology is certain to make this impossible. (Apart from the fact that Mr Sakaya's thesis rests on the nineteenth-century – and long disproven – belief that the Middle Ages spurned material goods. Alas, they lusted for them. They were obsessed with possessions and greedy beyond belief. There is substance to the old Marxist gibe that the Crusades were the biggest shopping trip ever. The Middle Ages were poor not because they chose to be poor. The Moslem conquest of the Hellenistic world and of the Mediterranean had cut off their access to antiquity's wealth producers.)

Still, redemption, self-renewal, spiritual growth, goodness and virtue – the 'New Man' to use the traditional term – are likely to be seen as *existential* rather than as a social goal and political pre-scription. The end of the belief in salvation by society surely marks an inward turning. It makes renewed emphasis on the individual, the person. It may even lead – at least we can so hope – to a return to individual responsibility.

The Third World

This book focuses on the developed countries – on Europe, on the United States and Canada, on Japan and the newly developed countries on the mainland of Asia, rather than on the developing countries of the 'Third World'. This is not because I consider the less-developed nations unimportant or even less important. That would be folly. Two-thirds of the world's population live, after all, in the Third World; and by the time the present period of transition comes to an end – around 2010 or 2020 – the Third World will house three-quarters. But I also consider it highly probable that within the next decade or two there will be new and startling 'economic miracles', in which poor, backward, Third-World countries transform themselves, virtually overnight, into fast-growth economic powers. It is even possible that there will be far more such transformations than there have been in the last 40 years, that is, since we first began to talk about 'economic development'. All the elements for rapid economic growth are present in the coastal, urbanized, areas of mainland China – from Tsientsin in the north to Canton in the south. They have a huge domestic market; a highly educated population with tremendous respect for learning; an old entrepreneurial tradition; close ties to the 'Overseas Chinese' in Singapore, Hong Kong and Taiwan, with access to their capital, their trading networks and their knowledgeable people. All this might be released in an explosion of entrepreneurial growth if Beijing's political and economic tyranny could be peacefully removed. Latin America's larger countries offer an adequate domestic market. Mexico may already be in the 'take-off' stage. And Brazil might surprise everybody by the speed of its turnaround once it musters the political courage to follow Mexico's recent example and abandon the failed (and indeed suicidal) policies into which it plunged after 1970. No one can possibly foretell what surprises the former Communist countries of Eastern Europe might produce.

But the developed countries also have a tremendous stake in the Third World. Unless there is rapid development there – both economic and social – the developed countries will be inundated by a human flood of Third-World immigrants far beyond their economic, social or cultural capacity to absorb them.

But the forces that are creating post-capitalist society and post-capitalist polity originate in the developed world. They are the product and result of its development. Answers to the challenges of post-capitalist society and post-capitalist polity will not be found in the Third World. If anything has been totally disproven it is the promises of the Third-World leaders of the 1950s and 1960s – Nehru in India, Mao in China, Castro in Cuba, Tito in Yugoslavia, the apostles of '*Négritude*' in Africa or Neo-Marxists like Che Guevara. They promised that the Third World would find new and different answers, and would indeed, create a new order. The Third World has not delivered on these promises made in its name. The challenges, the opportunities, the problems of post-capitalist society and post-capitalist polity can only be dealt with where they originated. And that is the developed world.

Society – polity – knowledge

This book covers a wide range. It deals with post-capitalist society; with post-capitalist polity; and with new challenges to knowledge itself. Yet it leaves out much more than it attempts to cover. It is not 'A History of the Future'. *It is a look at the present.*

The areas of discussion – Society; Polity; Knowledge – are not arrayed in order of importance. That would have put first the short discussion of the Educated Person which concludes this volume. The three areas are arrayed *in order of predictability.* In respect to the post-capitalist *society* we know what has happened and why; we know what is going to happen and why – at least in outline; and a good deal is already happening. In respect to the post-capitalist *polity* we only have programmes so far. How the needed changes will be brought about is still conjecture. But we know what has happened and why; we can specify what needs to happen and why. In respect to the *knowledge* challenges, however, we can only ask questions – and hope that they are the right questions.

I am often asked whether I am an optimist or a pessimist. For any survivor of this century to be an optimist would be fatuous. We surely are nowhere near the end of the turbulences, the transformations, the sudden upsets which have made this century one of the meanest, cruellest, bloodiest in human history. Anyone who deludes himself that we are anywhere near the 'end of history' is in for unpleasant surprises – the kind of surprises that afflicted America's President Bush when he first bet on the survival of the Russian Empire under Mikhail Gorbachev and then on the success of Boris Yeltsin's 'Commonwealth of Ex-Russian Nations'.

Nothing 'post' is permanent or even long-lived. Ours is a transition period. What the future society will look like, let alone whether it will indeed be the 'knowledge society' some of us dare hope for, depends how the developed countries respond to the challenges of this transition period, the post-capitalist period – their intellectual leaders, their business leaders, their political leaders, but above all each of us in our own work and life. But surely this is a time to *make the future* – precisely because everything is in flux. This is a time for *action*.

Part One

Society

1

From capitalism to knowledge society

Within 150 years, from 1750 to 1900, capitalism and technology conquered the globe and created a world civilization. Neither capitalism nor technical innovations were new; both had been common, recurrent phenomena throughout the ages, both in West and East. What was brand new was their speed of diffusion and their global reach across cultures, classes and geography. And it was this, their speed and scope, that converted capitalism into 'Capitalism' and into a 'system'. It converted technical advances into the 'Industrial Revolution'.

This transformation was driven by a radical change in the meaning of knowledge. In both West and East knowledge had always been seen as applying to *being*. Almost overnight, it came to be applied to *doing*. It became a resource and a utility. Knowledge had always been a private good. Almost overnight it became a public good.

For a hundred years – in the first phase – knowledge was applied to *tools, processes, products*. This created the Industrial Revolution. But it also created what Marx called 'alienation' and new classes and class war, and with it Communism. In its second phase, beginning around 1880 and culminating around World War II, knowledge in its new meaning came to be applied to *work*.

This ushered in the *Productivity Revolution* which in 75 years converted the proletarian into a middle-class bourgeois with near-upper-class income. The Productivity Revolution thus defeated class war and Communism. The last phase began after World War II. Knowledge is being applied to *knowledge* itself. This is the *Management Revolution*. Knowledge is now fast becoming the *one* factor of production, sidelining both capital and labour. It may be premature (and certainly would be presumptuous) to call ours a 'knowledge society' – so far we only have a knowledge economy. But our society is surely 'post-capitalist'.

Capitalism, in one form or another, has occurred and recurred many times throughout the ages, and in the Orient as well as in the West. And there have been many earlier periods of rapid technical invention and innovation, again in the Orient as well as in the West, many of them producing technical changes fully as radical as any in the late eighteenth or early nineteenth centuries.* What is unprecedented and unique about the developments of the last 250 years is their speed and scope. Instead of being one element in society as all earlier capitalism had been, Capitalism – with a capital C – became society. Instead of being confined, as always before, to a narrow locality, Capitalism – again with a capital C – took over all of Western and Northern Europe, in a short 100 years from 1750 to 1850. Then within another 50 years it took over the entire inhabited world.

All earlier capitalism had been confined to small narrow groups in society. Nobles, land-owners and the military, peasants, professionals, craftsmen, even labourers, were almost untouched by it.

* The best discussion of capitalism as a recurrent and fairly frequent phenomenon are two books by the great French economic historian, Fernand Braudel: *The Mediterranean* (2 vols) (first published in France in 1949; English translation New York: Harper & Row, 1972); and *Civilization & Capitalism* (3 vols) (first published in France in 1979, English translation New York: Harper & Row, 1981). The best discussions of earlier 'industrial revolutions' are *Medieval Technology and Social Change* by Lynn White Jr (Oxford University Press, 1962); *The Medieval Machine; The Industrial Revolution of the Middle Ages* by Jean Gimpel (first published in France in 1975; English translation New York: Holt Rinehart & Winston, 1976); and the monumental *Science & Civilization in China* by the British biochemist, orientalist and historian Joseph Needham (Cambridge University Press), publication of which began in 1954 with half of the planned 25 parts yet to appear. What Needham has published so far has, however, already completely changed our knowledge of early technology. For earlier 'industrial revolutions' see also my book *Technology Management & Society* (London: Heinemann, 1973), especially Chapters 3, 7 and 11.

Capitalism with a capital C soon permeated and transformed all groups in society wherever it spread.

From earliest times in the Old War new tools, new processes, new materials, new crops, new techniques – what we now call 'technology' – diffused swiftly.

Few modern inventions, for instance, spread as fast as a thirteenth-century one; eyeglasses. Derived from the optical experiments of an English Franciscan friar, Roger Bacon (died 1292 or 1294) around 1270, reading glasses for the elderly were in use at the Papal Court of Avignon by 1290, at the Sultan's Court in Cairo by 1300 and at the Court of the Mongol Emperor of China no later than 1310. Only the sewing machine and the telephone, fastest-spreading of all nineteenth-century inventions, moved as quickly.

But earlier technological change, almost without exception, remained confined to one craft or one application. It took another 200 years – until the early 1500s – before Bacon's invention had its second application: eyeglasses to correct nearsightedness. The potter's wheel was in full use in the Mediterranean by 1500 BC. Pots to cook, and to store water and food, were used in every household. Yet the principle underlying the potter's wheel was not applied until AD 1000 to women's work – spinning.

Similarly, the redesign of the windmill around the year AD 800 which converted it from the toy it had been in Antiquity into a true machine – and a fully 'automated' one at that – was not applied to ships for more than 300 years, that is, until after 1100. Until then, ships were oared; if wind was used at all to propel them, it was an auxiliary and only if it blew in the right direction. The sail to drive a ship works in exactly the same way as the sail that drives the windmill. The need for a sail that would enable a ship to sail cross-wind and against the wind had been known for a long time. The windmill was redesigned in Northern France or in the Low Countries, that is, in regions thoroughly familiar with ships and navigation. Yet it did not occur to anyone for several hundred years to apply something invented to pump water and to grind corn, that is, for use on land, to use offshore.

The inventions of the Industrial Revolution, however, were immediately applied across the board, and across all conceivable crafts and industries. They were immediately seen as *technology*.

James Watt's (1736-1819) redesign of the steam engine between 1765 and 1776 made it into a cost-effective provider of power.

Watt himself throughout his own productive life focused on one use only: to pump water out of a mine – the use for which the steam engine had first been designed by Newcomen in the early years of the eighteenth century. But one of England's leading iron masters immediately saw that the redesigned steam engine could also be used to blow air into a blast furnace and bid for the second engine Watt had built. And Watt's partner, Matthew Boulton (1728–1809), right away promoted the steam engine as a provider of power for all kinds of industrial processes, especially, of course, for the then largest of all manufacturing industries, textiles. Thirty-five years later, an American, Robert Fulton (1765–1815), floated the first steamship on New York's Hudson River. Another 20 years later the steam engine was put on wheels and the loco-motive was born. And by 1840 – at the latest by 1850 – the steam engine had transformed every single manufacturing process – from glass making to printing. It had transformed long-distance transportation on land and sea, and it was beginning to transform farming. By then, it had penetrated almost the entire world – with Tibet, Nepal and the interior of tropical Africa the only excep-tions.

The nineteenth century believed – and most people still do – that the Industrial Revolution was the first time a change in the 'mode of production' (to use Karl Marx's term) changed social structure and created new classes, the capitalist and the proletar-ian. But this belief too is not valid. Between AD 700 and 1000 two brand-new classes were created in Europe by technological change: the feudal knight and the urban craftsman. The knight was created by the invention of the stirrup – an invention coming out of Central Asia around the year AD 700; the craftsman by the redesign of water wheel and windmill into true machines which, for the first time, used inanimate forces – water and wind – as motive power rather than human muscle as Antiquity had done.

The stirrup made it possible to fight on horseback; without it a rider wielding a lance, sword or heavy bow would immediately have been thrown off the horse by the force of Newton's Second Law: 'To every action there is a reaction.' For several hundred years the knight was an invincible 'fighting machine'. But this machine had to be supported by a 'military-agricultural complex' – something quite new in history. Germans until this century called it a *Rittergut*, a knight's estate endowed with legal status and with economic and political privileges, and containing at least 50 peasant families or 200 people to produce the food needed to support the fighting machine: the knight, his squire, his three horses and his twelve to fifteen grooms. The stirrup, in other words, created feudalism.

The craftsman of Antiquity had been a slave. The craftsman of the first 'machine age', the craftsman of Europe's Middle Ages, became the urban ruling class, the 'burgher', who then created Europe's unique city, and both the Gothic and the Renaissance.

The technical innovations – stirrup, water wheel and windmill – travelled throughout the entire Old World, and fast. But the classes of the earlier industrial revolution remained European phenomena on the whole. Only Japan evolved around AD 1100 proud and independent craftsmen who enjoyed high esteem and, until 1600, considerable power. But while the Japanese adopted the stirrup for riding they continued to fight on foot. The rulers in rural Japan were the commanders of foot soldiers – the *daimyo*. They levied taxes on the peasantry but had no feudal estates. In China, in India, in the world of Islam, the new technologies had no social impact whatever. Craftsmen in China remained serfs without social status. The military did not become land-owners but remained, as in Europe's Antiquity, professional mercenaries. Even in Europe the social changes generated by this early industrial revolution took almost 400 years to have a full effect.

By contrast, the social transformation of society brought about by Capitalism and Industrial Revolution took less than a hundred years to become fully effective in Western Europe. In 1750 capitalists and proletarians were still marginal groups. In fact, proletarians in the nineteenth-century meaning of the term (that is, factory workers) hardly existed at all. By 1850 capitalists and proletarians were the dynamic classes of Western Europe, and were on the offensive. They rapidly became the dominant classes wherever capitalism and modern technology penetrated. In Japan the transformation took less than 30 years, from the Meiji Restoration in 1867 to the war with China in 1894. It took not much longer in Shanghai and Hong Kong, Calcutta and Bombay, or in the Tsar's Russia.

Capitalism and the Industrial Revolution – because of their speed and of their scope – created a world civilization.*

* The best history of this development is *Prometheus Unbound* by the Harvard historian David S. Landes (Cambridge University Press, 1969).

The new meaning of knowledge

Unlike those 'terrible simplifiers', the nineteenth-century ideologues such as Hegel and Marx, we now know that major historical events rarely have just one cause and just one explanation. They typically result from the convergence of a good many separate and independent developments.

One example of how history works is the genesis of the computer. Its earliest root is the binary system, that is, the realization of a seventeenth-century mathematician-philosopher, the German Gottfried Leibnitz (1646–1716), that *all* numbers can be represented by just two: 0 and 1. The second root is the discovery of a nineteenth-century English inventor, Charles Babbage (1792–1871), that toothed wheels (that is, mechanics) could represent the arithmetic functions: addition, subtraction, multiplication and division – the discovery of a genuine 'computing machine'. Then in the early years of this century, two English logicians Alfred North Whitehead (1861–1947) and Bertrand Russell (1872–1970), in their *Principia Mathematica*, showed that any concept if presented in rigorously logical form can be expressed mathematically. From this discovery an Austro-American, Otto Neurath (flourished 1915–1930), working as statistician for the US War Production Board of World War I, derived 'data', that is, the idea, then brand-new and heretical, that all information from any area, whether anatomy or astronomy, economics, history, or zoology, is exactly the same when quantified, and can be treated and presented the same way (the idea, by the way, that also underlies modern statistics). A little earlier, just before World War I, an American, Lee de Forest (1873–1961), invented the audion tube to convert electronic impulses into sound waves, thus making possible the broadcasting of speech and music. Twenty years later it occurred to engineers working at a medium-sized punch-card manufacturer called IBM that the audion tube could be used to switch electronically from 0 to 1 and back again. If any of these elements had been missing there would have been no computer. And no one can say which of these was *the* element. With all of them in place, however, the computer became virtually inevitable. It was then pure accident, however, that it became an American development – the accident of World War II which made the American military willing to spend enormous sums on developing (quite unsuccessfully, by the way, until well after World War II) machines to calculate at high speed the position of fast-moving aircraft overhead and of fast-moving enemy ships. Otherwise the computer would probably have become a British development. Indeed, an English company, the food producer and restaurant owner J. Lyons & Co., in the 1940s actually developed the first computer for commercial purpose that really worked, the '*Leo*' – Lyons just couldn't raise the money to compete with the Pentagon and had to abandon its working and successful (and very much cheaper) machine.

Similarly, many separate developments – most of them probably quite unconnected with each other – went into making capitalism into Capitalism and technical advance into the Industrial Revolution. The best-known theory – that Capitalism was the child of the 'Protestant Ethic' – expounded in the opening years of this century by the German sociologist Max Weber (1864–1920) – has, however, been largely discredited. There just is not enough evidence for it. There is only a little more evidence to support Karl Marx's earlier thesis that the steam engine, the new prime mover, required such enormous capital investment that craftsmen could no longer finance their 'means of production', and had to cede control to the capitalist. There is one critical element, however, without which well-known phenomena, i.e. capitalism and technical advance, could not possibly have turned into a social and worldwide pandemic. It is the radical change in the *meaning of knowledge* that occurred in Europe around the year 1700, or shortly thereafter.*

There are as many theories as to what we can know and how we can know it as there have been metaphysicians from Plato in 400 BC to Ludwig Wittgenstein (1889–1951) and Karl Popper (1902–) in our days. But since Plato's days there have only been two theories in the West – and since somewhat the same time, two theories in the East – regarding the meaning and function of knowledge. Plato's spokesman, the wise Socrates, holds that the only function of knowledge is self-knowledge, that is, the intellectual, moral and spiritual growth of the person. His ablest

---

* This change is explored in some depth in my 1961 essay: 'The Technological Revolution; Notes on the Relationship of Technology, Science and Culture', reprinted in my 1973 essay volume *Technology, Management and Society* (London: Heinemann) and in my 1992 essay volume *The Ecological Vision* (New Brunswick, NJ: Transaction Publishers).

opponent, the brilliant and learned Protagoras, holds, however, that the purpose of knowledge is to make the holder effective by enabling him to know what to say and how to say it. For Protagoras knowledge meant logic, grammar and rhetoric – later to become the *trivium*, the core of learning in the Middle Ages – and still very much what we mean by a 'liberal education' or what the Germans mean by *Allgemeine Bildung*. In the East there were pretty much the same two theories of knowledge. Knowledge for the Confucian was knowing what to say and how to say it and the way to advancement and earthly success. Knowledge for the Taoist and the Zen monk was self-knowledge and the road to enlightenment and wisdom. But while the two sides thus sharply disagreed about what knowledge means, they were in total agreement as to what it did *not* mean. It did not mean *ability to do*. It did not mean *utility*. Utility was not knowledge; it was *skill* – the Greek word is *téchne*.

Unlike their Far Eastern contemporaries, the Chinese Confucians with their infinite contempt for anything but book learning, both Socrates and Protagoras respected *téchne*.

In fact, in the West contempt for skill was unknown until England's eighteenth-century 'gentleman'. And this contempt which reached such heights in Victorian England was surely little but a futile last-ditch defence against the gentleman's being replaced as society's ruling group by capitalist and technologist.

But even to Socrates and Protagoras, *téchne*, however commendable, was not knowledge. It was confined to one specific application and had no general principles. What the shipmaster knew about navigating from Greece to Sicily could not be applied to anything else. Furthermore, the only way to learn a *téchne* was through apprenticeship and experience. A *téchne* could not be explained in words, whether spoken or written. It could only be demonstrated. As late as 1700, or even later, the English did not speak of 'crafts'. They spoke of 'mysteries' – and not only because the possessor of a craft skill was sworn to secrecy but also because a craft, by definition, was inaccessible to anyone who had not been apprenticed to a master and had thus been taught by example.

The Industrial Revolution

Then, beginning after 1700 – and within an incredibly short 50 years – technology was invented. The very word is a manifesto in that it combined *téchne*, that is, the mystery of a craft skill, with *logy*, that is, organized, systematic, purposeful knowledge. The first engineering school, the French *Ecole des Ponts et Chaussées*, was founded in 1747, followed around 1770 in Germany by the first School of Agriculture and in 1776 by the first School of Mining. In 1794 the first technical university, the French *Ecole Polytechnique*, was founded, and with it, the profession of engineer. Shortly thereafter, between 1820 and 1850, medical education and medical practice were reorganized as a systematic technology.

In a parallel development, Britain, between 1750 and 1800, shifted from patents being monopolies to enrich royal favourites to patents being granted to encourage the application of knowledge to tools, products and processes, and to reward inventors provided they publish their inventions. This not only triggered a century of feverish mechanical invention in Britain; it finished craft mystery and secretiveness.

The great document of this dramatic shift from skill to technology – one of the most important books in history – was the *Encyclopédie*, edited between 1751 and 1772 by Denis Diderot (1713–1784) and Jean d'Alembert (1717–1783). This famous work attempted to bring together in organized and systematic form the knowledge of all crafts, and in such a way that the non-apprentice could learn to be a 'technologist'. It was by no means accidental that articles in the *Encyclopédie* that describe an individual craft (e.g. spinning or weaving) were not written by craftsmen. They were written by 'information specialists': people trained as analysts, as mathematicians, as logicians – both Voltaire and Rousseau were contributors. The underlying thesis of the *Encyclopédie* was that effective results in the material universe – in tools, processes and products – are produced by systematic analysis, and by systematic, purposeful application of knowledge.

But the *Encyclyopédie* also preached that principles which produced results in one craft would produce results in any other. That was anathema, however, to both the traditional man of knowledge and the traditional craftsman.

None of the technical schools of the eighteenth century aimed at producing *new* knowledge – nor did the *Encyclopédie*. None even talked of the application of *science* to tools, processes and products, that is, to technology. This idea had to wait for another hundred years until 1840 or so, when a German chemist, Justus Liebig (1803–1873), applied science to invent first, artificial fertilizers and then a way to preserve animal protein, the meat extract. What the early technical schools and the *Encyclopédie* did was, however, more important perhaps. They brought together, codified and *published* the *téchne*, the craft mystery, as it had been developed over millennia. They converted experience into knowledge, apprenticeship into textbook, secrecy into methodology, doing into applied knowledge. These are the essentials of what we have come to call the 'Industrial Revolution', i.e. the transformation by technology of society and civilization worldwide.

It is this change in the meaning of knowledge which then made modern Capitalism inevitable and dominant. The speed of technical change created demand for capital way beyond anything the craftsman could possibly supply. The new technology also required concentration of production, that is, the shift to the factory. Knowledge could not be applied in thousands and tens of thousands of small individual workshops and in the cottage industries of the rural village. It required concentration of production under one roof.

The new technology also required large-scale energy, whether water power or steam power, which could not be decentralized. But, though important, these energy needs were secondary. The central point was that production almost overnight moved from being craft based to being technology based. As a result, the capitalist moved almost overnight into the centre of economy and society. Before, he had always been 'supporting cast'.

As late as 1750, large-scale enterprise was governmental rather than private. The earliest and for many centuries the greatest of all manufacturing enterprises in the Old World was the famous arsenal owned and run by the government of Venice. And the eighteenth-century 'manufactories' such as the procelain works of Meissen and Sèvres were still government-owned. But by 1830 large-scale private capitalist enterprise dominated in the West. Another 50 years later, by the time Karl Marx died in 1883, private capitalist enterprise had penetrated everywhere except to such remote corners of the world as Tibet or the Empty Quarter of Arabia.

There was resistance, of course, both to technology and to capitalism. There were riots, in England for instance, or in German Silesia. But these were local, lasted a few weeks or at most a few months, and did not even slow down the speed and spread of Capitalism.

The Industrial Revolution, that is, the machine and the factory system, spread equally fast and equally without meeting much resistance, if any.

Adam Smith's (1723–1790) *Wealth of Nations* appeared in the same year (1776) in which James Watt patented the perfected steam engine. Yet the *Wealth of Nations* pays practically no attention to machines or factories or industrial production altogether. The production it describes is still craft based. Even 40 years later after the Napoleonic Wars, factories and machines were not yet seen as central even by acute social observers. They play practically no role in the economics of David Ricardo (1772–1832). Even more surprising, neither factory nor factory workers nor bankers can be found in the books of Jane Austen (1775–1817), England's most perceptive social critic. Her society (as has often been said) is thoroughly 'bourgeois'. But it is still totally pre-industrial, a society of squires and tenants, parsons and naval officers, lawyers, craftsmen and shopkeepers. Only in far-away America did Alexander Hamilton (1757–1809) see very early that machine-based manufacturing was fast becoming the central economic activity. But few even among his followers paid much attention to his 1791 *Report on Manufactures* until long after his death.

By the 1830s, however, Honoré de Balzac (1799–1850) was turning out best-selling novel after best-selling novel depicting a capitalist France whose society was dominated by bankers and by the stock exchange. And another 15 years later, capitalism, the factory system, the machine, are central in the mature works of Charles Dickens (1812–1870), and so are the new classes, the capitalists and the proletarians.

In *Bleak House* (1852) the new society and its tensions form the sub-plot in the contrast between two able brothers, both sons of the squire's housekeeper. One becomes a great industrialist in the North who plans to get himself elected to Parliament to fight the land-owners and break their power. The other chooses to remain a loyal retainer of the broken, defeated, ineffectual (but pre-capitalist) 'gentleman'. And Dickens's *Hard Times* (1854) is the first and by far the most powerful industrial novel, the story of a bitter strike in a cotton mill and of class war at its starkest.

This unheard of speed with which society was transformed created the social tensions and conflicts of the new order. We now know that there is no truth in the all but universal belief that factory workers in the early nineteenth century were worse off and were treated more harshly then they had been as landless labourers in the pre-industrial countryside. They were badly off, no doubt, and harshly treated. But they flocked to the factory precisely because they were still better off than they were at the bottom of a static, tyrannical and starving rural society. They still experienced a much better 'quality of life'.

We should have known this all along, by the way. In the factory town infant mortality immediately went down and life expectancies immediately went up, thus triggering the enormous population growth of industrializing Europe. But now, that is, since World War II, we also have the example of the Third-World countries. Brazilians and Peruvians stream into the *favelas* and *barrios* of Rio de Janeiro and Lima. However hard, life there is better than in the impoverished *Noreste* of Brazil or on Peru's *Altiplano*. Indians today say: 'The poorest beggar in Bombay still eats better than the farm hand in the village.' 'England's green and pleasant land' which William Blake (1757–1827) in his famous poem on the 'New Jerusalem' hoped to liberate from the new 'satanic mills' was in reality one vast rural slum.

But while industrialization thus, from the beginning, meant material improvement rather than Marx's famous 'immiseration', the speed of change was so breathtaking as to be deeply traumatic. The new class, the 'proletarians', became 'alienated', to use the term Marx coined. Their alienation, Marx predicted, would make inevitable their exploitation. For they were becoming totally dependent for their livelihood on access to the 'means of production' which were owned and controlled by the capitalist. This then, Marx predicted, would increasingly concentrate ownership in fewer and bigger hands and increasingly impoverish a powerless proletariat – until the day on which the system would collapse under its own weight, with the few remaining capitalists being overthrown by proletarians who 'had nothing to lose but their chains'.

We now know that Marx was a false prophet – the very opposite of what he predicted has in fact happened. But this is hindsight. Most of his contemporaries shared his view of capitalism even if they did not necessarily share his prediction of the outcome. Even anti-Marxists accepted Marx's analysis of the 'inherent contradictions of capitalism'. Some were confident that the military would keep the proletarian rabble in check as was apparently the greatest of nineteenth-century capitalists, the American banker J. P. Morgan (1837–1913). Liberals of all stripes believed that somehow there could be reform and amelioration. But the conviction that capitalist society was a society of inevitable class conflict, practically every thinking person of the late nineteenth-century shared with Marx – and in fact by 1910 most 'thinking people', at least in Europe (but also in Japan), were inclining towards Socialism. The greatest of nineteenth-century Conservatives, Benjamin Disraeli (1804–1881), saw capitalist society very much as Marx did. So did his conservative counterpart on the Continent, Otto von Bismarck (1815–1898); it motivated him, after 1880, to enact the social legislation that produced ultimately the twentieth-century Welfare State. The conservative social critic, the American novelist Henry James (1843–1916), chronicler of American wealth and European aristocracy, was so obsessed by class war and by the fear of class war that he made it the theme of his most haunting novel *The Princess Casamassima*. He wrote it in 1883, the very year of Marx's death.

The Productivity Revolution

What then defeated Marx and Marxism? By 1950 a good many of us already knew that Marxism had failed both morally and economically (I had said so already in 1939 in my book *The End of Economic Man*). But Marxism was still the one coherent ideology for most of the world. And for most of the world it looked invincible. There were 'anti-Marxists' galore, but, as yet, few 'non-Marxists', that is, people who thought that Marxism had become irrelevant – as most of the world now knows. Even those bitterly opposed to Socialism were still convinced that it was in the ascendant.

The father of Neo-conservatism throughout the Western world, the Anglo-Austrian economist Friedrich von Hayek (1899–1992), in his 1944 book *The Road to Serfdom* argued that Socialism would inevitably mean enslavement. There is, Hayek then said, no such thing as 'Democratic Socialism'; there is only 'Totalitarian Socialism'. But Hayek did not argue in 1944 that Marxism *could* not work. On the contrary, he was very much afraid that it could and would work. But his last book, *The Fatal Conceit* (University of Chicago Press, 1988) written 40 years later, argues that Marxism could never have worked. And by the time he published this book almost everybody – and especially almost everybody in the Communist countries – had already come to the same conclusion.

What then overcame the 'inevitable contradictions of capitalism', the 'alienation' and 'immiseration' of the proletarians and with it the 'proletarian' altogether.

The answer is the *Productivity Revolution*.

When knowledge changed its meaning 250 years ago it began to be applied to tools, processes and products. This is still what 'technology' means to most people and what is being taught in engineering schools. But two years before Marx's death the Productivity Revolution had begun. In 1881 an American, Frederick Winslow Taylor (1856–1915), first applied knowledge to the study of *work*, the analysis of work and the engineering of work.

Work has been around as long as man. All animals in fact have to work for their living. And in the West the dignity of work has been paid lip service for a long time.

The second oldest Greek text, following the Homeric epics by only a hundred years or so, is a poem by Hesiod (eighth century BC) entitled *Works and Days*, which sings of the work of the farmer. One of the finest Roman poems is Virgil's (70–19 BC) *Georgics*, a cycle of songs about the work of the farmer. Although there is no such concern with work in the Eastern literary tradition, the Emperor of China once a year touched a plough to celebrate rice planting.

But both in the West and in the East, these were purely symbolic gestures. Neither Hesiod nor Virgil actually looked at what a farmer *does*. Nor did anybody else throughout most of recorded history.* Work was beneath the attention of educated people, of well-to-do people, of people of authority. Work is what slaves did.

---

* And there still is no history of work – but then also, despite all the philosophizing about knowledge, there is no history of knowledge either. Both should become important areas of study within the next decades or at least within the next century.

'Everybody knew' that the only way a worker could produce more was by working longer hours or by working harder. Marx too shared this belief with every other nineteenth-century economist or engineer.

It was pure accident that Frederick Winslow Taylor, a well-to-do, educated man, became a worker. Poor eyesight forced him to give up going to Harvard and to take instead a worker's job in an iron foundry. Being extremely gifted, Taylor very soon rose to be one of the bosses. And his metal-working inventions made him a rich man very early. What then got Taylor to start on the study of work was his shock at the mutual and growing hatred between capitalists and workers, which had come to dominate the late nineteenth century. Taylor, in other words, saw what Marx saw and Disraeli and Bismarck and Henry James. But he also saw what they failed to see: the conflict was unnecessary. He set out to make workers productive so that they would earn decent money.

Taylor's motivation was not efficiency. It was not the creation of profits for the owners. To his very death he maintained that the major beneficiary of the fruits of productivity had to be the worker and not the owner. His main motivation was the creation of a society in which owners and workers, capitalists and proletarians had a common interest in productivity and could build a relationship of harmony on the application of knowledge to work. The ones who have come closest to understanding this so far are Japan's post-World War II employers and Japan's post-World War II unions.

Few figures in intellectual history have had greater impact than Taylor. And few have been so wilfully misunderstood and so assiduously misquoted.* In part, Taylor has suffered because history has proven him right and the intellectuals wrong. In part, Taylor is ignored because contempt for work still lingers, above all among the intellectuals. Surely shovelling sand – the most publicized of Taylor's analyses – is not something an 'educated man' would appreciate let alone consider important.

In much larger part, however, Taylor's reputation has suffered precisely because he applied knowledge to the study of work. This was anathema to the labour unions of his day; and they

* In fact, no factually reliable biography was published until 1991, when *Frederick W. Taylor; Myth and Reality* by Charles D. Wrege and Ronald J. Greenwood appeared (Homewood, Illinois: Irwin).

mounted against Taylor one of the most vicious campaigns of character assassination in American history.

Taylor's crime, in the eyes of the unions, was his assertion that there is no 'skilled work'. In manual operations there is only 'work'. All can be analysed the same way. Any worker who is then willing to do the work the way analysis shows it should be done is a 'first-class man', deserving a 'first-class wage' – that is, as much or more than the skilled worker got with his long years of apprenticeship.

But the unions that were respected and powerful in Taylor's America were the unions in the government-owned arsenals and shipyards in which, prior to World War I, all peace-time defence production was done in the United States. These unions were craft monopolies. Membership of them was restricted to sons or relatives of members. They required an apprenticeship of five to seven years but had no systematic training or work study. Nothing was allowed ever to be written down. There were not even blueprints or any other drawings of the work to be done. The members were sworn to secrecy and were not permitted to discuss their work with non-members. Taylor's assertion that work could be studied, could be analysed, could be divided into a series of simple repetitive motions each of which had to be done in its one right way, its own best time, and with its own right tools was indeed a frontal attack on them. And so they vilified him and succeeded in having Congress ban task study in government arsenals and shipyards, a ban that prevailed until after World War II.

Taylor did not improve matters by offending the owners of his day as much as he offended the unions. While he had little use for unions he was contemptuously hostile to the owners; his favourite epithet for them was 'hogs'. And then there was his insistence that the workers rather than the owners should get the lion's share of the revenue gains scientific management produced. To add insult to injury: his 'Fourth Principle' demanded that work study be done in consultation, if not in partnership, with the worker. Finally, Taylor held that authority in the plant must not be based on ownership. It could be based only on superior knowledge. He demanded, in other words, what we now call 'professional management' – and that was anathema and 'radical heresy' to nineteenth-century capitalists. He was bitterly attacked by them as a 'trouble-maker' and a 'socialist'. (Some of his closest disciples and associates, especially Karl Barth, Taylor's right-hand man, were indeed open and avowed 'leftists' and strongly anti-capitalist.)

Taylor's axiom that all manual work, skilled or unskilled, could be analysed and organized by the application of knowledge seemed preposterous to his contemporaries. And that there is a mystique to craft skill was universally accepted for many, many years.

This belief still encouraged Hitler in 1941 to declare war on the United States. For the latter to field an effective force in Europe would require a large fleet to transport troops. America at that time had almost no merchant marine and no destroyers to protect it. Modern war, Hitler further argued, required precision optics and in large quantities; and there were no skilled optical workers in America.

Hitler was absolutely right. The United States did not have much of a merchant marine and its destroyers were few and ludicrously obsolete. It also had almost no optical industry. But by applying Taylor's 'task study' the United States learned how to train totally unskilled workers, many of them former sharecroppers raised in a pre-industrial environment, and converted them in 60 or 90 days into first-rate welders and shipbuilders. The United States equally trained within a few months the same kind of people to turn out precision optics of better quality than the Germans ever did – and on an assembly line to boot.

Altogether, where Taylor had the greatest impact was probably in training.

Adam Smith, only a hundred years earlier, had taken for granted that it takes at least 50 years of experience (and more likely a full century) until a country or a region has acquired the necessary skills to turn out high-quality products – his examples were the production of musical instruments in Bohemia and Saxony, and of silk fabrics in Scotland. Seventy years later, around 1840, a German, August Borsig (1804–1854) – one of the first people outside England to build a steam locomotive – invented what is still the German system of apprenticeship which combines practical plant experience under a master with theoretical grounding in school. It is still the foundation of German's industrial productivity. But even Borsig's apprenticeship took three to five years. Then, first in World War I but especially in World War II, the United States systematically applied Taylor's approach to training 'first-class men' in a few months. This, more than any other factor, explains why the United States could mount the war production which ultimately defeated both Japan and Germany.

All earlier economic powers in modern history – England, the United States, Germany – emerged through leadership in new technology. The post-World War II economic powers – first Japan, then South Korea, Taiwan, Hong Kong, Singapore – all owe their rise to Taylor's training. It enabled them to endow a still largely pre-industrial and therefore still low-wage workforce with world-class productivity in practically no time. In the post-World War II decades Taylor-based training became the one truly effective engine of economic development.

The application of knowledge to work explosively increased productivity.* For hundreds of years there had been no increase in the ability of workers to turn out goods or to move goods. Machines created greater capacity. But workers themselves were no more productive than they had been in the workshops of ancient Greece, in building the roads of Imperial Rome or in producing the highly prized woollen cloth which gave Renaissance Florence its wealth.

But within a few years after Taylor began to apply knowledge to work, productivity began to rise at a rate of 3½–4% compound a year – which means doubling every 18 years or so. Since Taylor began, productivity has increased some fiftyfold in all advanced countries. On this unprecedented expansion rest all the increases in both standard of living and in the quality of life in developed countries.

Half of this additional productivity has been taken in the form of increased purchasing power, that is, in a higher standard of living. But between one-third and one-half has been taken in the form of increased leisure. As late as 1910 workers in developed countries still worked as much as they had ever worked before, that is, at least 3000 hours a year. By now even the Japanese work 2000 hours a year, the Americans around 1850, the Germans, at most, 1600 – and they all produce fifty times as much per hour as 80 years ago. Other substantial shares of the increased productivity have been taken in the form of health care, which has grown from something like 0% of Gross

---

* The term itself was unknown in Taylor's time. In fact, it was still unknown until before World War II, when it first began to be used in the United States. As late as 1950 the most authoritative English dictionary, the *Concise Oxford*, still did not list the term 'productivity' in its present meaning.

National Product (GNP) to 8–12% in developed countries, and in the form of education, which has grown from around 2% of GNP to 10% or more.

And most of this increase – as Taylor predicted – has been taken by the workers, that is, by Marx's proletarians. Henry Ford (1863–1947) brought out the first cheap car, the Model T in 1907. It was 'cheap', however, only by comparison with all other cars on the market which, in terms of average incomes, cost as much as a two-engine private plane today. At $750 Henry Ford's Model T cost what a fully employed industrial worker in the United States earned in three to four years – for then 80 cents was a good day's wage and, of course, there were no 'benefits'. Even an American physician in those days rarely earned more than $500 a year. Today, a unionized car worker in the United States, Japan or Germany, working only 40 hours a week, earns $50 000 in wages and benefits – $45 000 after taxes – which is roughly eight times what a cheap new car in the United States costs today.

By 1930 Taylor's Scientific Management – despite resistance by unions and by intellectuals – had swept the developed world. As a result Marx's 'proletarian' became a 'bourgeois'. The blue-collar worker in manufacturing industry, the 'proletarian', rather than the 'capitalist', became the true beneficiary of Capitalism and the Industrial Revolution. This explains the total failure of Marxism in the highly developed countries for which Marx had predicted 'revolution' by 1900. It explains why, after 1918, there was no 'Proletarian Revolution' even in the defeated countries of Central Europe in which there was misery, hunger and unemployment. It explains why the Great Depression did not lead to a Communist Revolution, as Lenin and Stalin – and practically all Marxists – had confidently expected. By that time, Marx's proletarians had not yet become 'affluent'. But they had already become middle class. They had become productive.

'Darwin, Marx, Freud' is the trinity often cited as the 'makers of the modern world'. Marx would be taken out and replaced by Taylor if there were any justice in the world. But that Taylor is not given his due is a minor matter. It *is* a serious matter, however, that far too few people realize that it is the application of knowledge to work which created developed economies by setting off the productivity explosion of the last hundred years. Technologists give the credit to machines, economists to capital investment. But both were as copious in the first hundred years of the capitalist age, that is, before 1880, as they have been since. In respect to technology or to capital, the second hundred years differed little from the first hundred. But there was absolutely no increase in worker productivity in the first hundred years – and consequently also little increase in workers' real incomes or any decrease in their working hours. What made the second hundred years so critically different can only be explained as the result of *applying knowledge to work.*

The productivity of the new classes, the classes of the post-capitalist society, can be increased *only* by applying knowledge to work. Neither machines nor capital can do it – indeed if applied alone they are likely to impede rather than to create productivity (as will be further discussed in Chapter 4).

When Taylor started, nine out of every ten working people did manual work, making or moving *things*; in manufacturing, in farming, in mining, in transportation. The productivity of people engaged in making and moving things is still going up at the historical rate of 3½–4% – and in American and French agriculture even faster. But the *Productivity Revolution* is over. Forty years ago, in the 1950s, people who engaged in work to make or to move things were still a majority in all developed countries. By 1990 they had shrunk to one-fifth of the workforce. By 2010 they will be no more than one-tenth. Increasing the productivity of manual workers in manufacturing, in farming, in mining, in transportation, can no longer by itself create wealth. The productivity revolution has become a victim of its own success. From now on what matters is the productivity of non-manual workers. And that requires *applying knowledge to knowledge.*

The Management Revolution

When I decided in 1926 not to go to college but to go to work after finishing secondary school, my father was quite distressed; ours had long been a family of lawyers and doctors. But he did not call me a 'drop-out'. He did not try to change my mind. And he did not prophesy that I would never amount to anything. I was a responsible adult wanting to work as an adult.*

---

* That I then also got a doctorate on the side had more to do with my trying to annoy my father than with any belief on my part that it would make any difference to my life and career.

Thirty years later, when my son reached age 18, I practically forced him to go to college. Like his father, he wanted to be an adult among adults. Like his father, he felt that in 12 years of sitting on a school bench he had learned little, and that his chances to learn much by spending four more years on a school bench were not particularly great. Like his father at that age, he was action-focused and not learning-focused.

And yet by 1958, 31 years after I had moved from being a high-school graduate to being a trainee in an export firm, the college degree had become a necessity. It had become the passport to practically all careers. Not to go to college in 1958 was 'dropping out' for an American boy who had grown up in a well-to-do family and who had done well in school. My father did not have the slightest difficulty in finding a trainee job for me in a reputable merchant house. Thirty years later such firms would not have accepted a high-school graduate as a trainee. They would all have said 'go to college for four years – and then you probably should go on to graduate school'.

In my father's generation – he was born in 1876 – going to college was either for the sons of the wealthy or for a very small number of poor but exceptionally brilliant youngsters (such as he had been).

Of all the American business successes of the nineteenth century, only one went to college: J. P. Morgan went to Göttingen to study mathematics but dropped out after one year. Few of the others even attended high school let alone graduated from it. In the novels of Edith Wharton, the chronicler of American society around 1910 to 1920, the sons of the old and rich New York families do go to Harvard and to Harvard Law School. But practially none of them then practises law. Higher education was a luxury and an ornament and a pleasant way to spend one's early adulthood.

By my time, going to college was already desirable. It gave social status. But it was by no means necessary nor very much of a help in one's life and career. When I did the first study of a major business corporation, General Motors,* the Public Relations Department at the company tried very hard to conceal the fact that a good many of their top executives had gone to college. The proper thing then was to start as a machinist and work one's way

* Published in my book *Concept of the Corporation* (1946).

up.* As late as 1950 or 1960, the quickest way to middle-class income – in the United States, in Britain, in Germany (though already no longer in Japan) – was *not* to go to college. It was to go to work at age 16 in one of the unionized mass-production industries. There one earned a middle-class income after a few months – the result of the productivity explosion. These opportunities are practically gone.† Now there is practically no access to middle-class income without a formal degree which certifies to the acquisition of knowledge that can only be obtained systematically and in a school.

The change in the meaning of knowledge that began 250 years ago has transformed society and economy. Formal knowledge is seen as both the key personal resource and the key economic resource. *Knowledge is the only meaningful resource today.* The traditional 'factors of production' – land (i.e. natural resources), labour and capital – have not disappeared. But they have become secondary. They can be obtained, and obtained easily, provided there is knowledge. And knowledge in this new meaning is knowledge as a utility, knowledge as the means to obtain social and economic results.

These developments, whether desirable or not, are responses to an irreversible change: *knowledge is now being applied to knowledge.* This is the third and perhaps the ultimate step in the transformation of knowledge. Supplying knowledge to find out how *existing* knowledge can best be applied to produce results is, in effect, what we mean by *management.* But knowledge is now also being applied systematically and purposefully to define what *new* knowledge is needed, whether it is feasible and what has to be done to make knowledge effective. It is being applied, in other words, to Systematic Innovation.‡

This third change in the dynamics of knowledge can be called the *Management Revolution.* Like its two predecessors – knowledge applied to tools, processes and products, and knowledge applied to human work – the Management Revolution has swept the Earth. It took a hundred years, from the middle of the eighteenth century to the middle of the nineteenth for the Industrial Revolution to become dominant and worldwide. It took some 70

---

* The story is told in the chapter 'Alfred P. Sloan' in my book *Adventures of a Bystander* (1980, reissued 1991).
    † On this see also Chapter 3, especially the section 'Is Labour Still an Asset?'
    ‡ On this, see my book *Innovation and Entrepreneurship* (1985).

years, from 1880 to the end of World War II, for the Productivity Revolution to become dominant and worldwide. It has taken less than 50 years – from 1945 to 1990 – for the Management Revolution to become dominant and worldwide.

Most people, when they hear the word 'management', still hear 'business management'. Management did first emerge in its present form in large-scale business organizations. When I first began to work on management some 50 years ago I too concentrated on business management.* But we soon learned that management is needed in all modern organizations, whether businesses or non-businesses. In fact, we soon learned that it is needed even *more* in organizations that are not businesses, whether not-for-profit but non-governmental organizations (what in this book I propose to call the 'Social Sector') or government agencies. These organizations need management the most precisely because they lack the discipline of the 'bottom line' under which business stands. That management is not confined to business was recognized first in the United States. But it is now becoming accepted in all developed countries (as witness the receptivity in Western Europe, Japan and Brazil to my 1990 book *Managing the Non Profit Organization*).

We now know that management is a generic function of all organizations, whatever their specific mission. It is the generic organ of the knowledge society.

Management has been around for a very long time. I am often asked whom I consider the best or the greatest executive. My answer is always 'the man who conceived, designed and built the first Egyptian Pyramid more than 4000 years ago – and it still stands'. But management as a specific kind of work was not seen until after World War I – and then by a handful of people only. Management as a discipline only emerged after World War II. As late as 1950 when the World Bank began to lend money for economic development, the word 'management' was not even in its vocabulary. In fact, while management was *invented* thousands of years ago it was not discovered until after World War II.

One reason for its discovery was the experience of World War II itself and especially the performance of American industry. But

* In my book *The Practice of Management*, which first established management as a discipline and which appeared in 1954, most of the discussion is of business management, and so are most examples.

perhaps equally important to the general acceptance of management has been the performance of Japan since 1950. Japan was not an 'underdeveloped' country after World War II. But its industry and economy were almost totally destroyed; and it had practically no domestic technology. The nation's main resource was its willingness to adopt and to adapt the management which the Americans had developed during World War II (and especially training). Within 20 years, from the 1950s, when the American occupation of Japan ended, to the 1970s, Japan became the world's second economic power and a technology leader.

When the Korean War ended in the early 1950s South Korea was destroyed even more than Japan had been seven years earlier. And it had never been anything but a backward country, especially as the Japanese systematically suppressed Korean enterprise and Korean higher education during their 35 years of occupation. But by using the colleges and universities of the United States to educate their able young people, and by importing and applying management South Korea became a highly developed country within 25 years.

With this powerful expansion of management came a growing understanding of what management really is. When I first began to study management, during and immediately after World War II,* a manager was defined as 'someone who is responsible for the work of subordinates'. A manager, in other words, was a 'boss', and management was rank and power. This is probably still the definition a good many people have in mind when they speak of managers and management.

But by the early 1950s, the definition had already changed to 'a manager is responsible for the performance of people'. Now we know that this also is too narrow a definition. The right definition is *'a manager is responsible for the application and performance of knowledge'*.

This change means that we now see knowledge as the essential resource. Land, labour and capital are chiefly important as restraints. Without them even knowledge cannot produce. Without them even management cannot perform. Where there is effective management, that is, application of knowledge to knowledge, we can always obtain the other resources.

That knowledge has become *the* resource, rather than *a* resource

* On this, see my 1946 book, *Concept of the Corporation*.

is what makes our society 'post-capitalist'. It changes, and fundamentally, the structure of society. It creates new social dynamics. It
creates new economic dynamics. It creates new politics.

From knowledge to knowledges

Underlying all three phases in the shift to knowledge – the
Industrial Revolution, the Productivity Revolution, the Management Revolution – is a fundamental change in the meaning of
knowledge. We have moved from knowledge to knowledges.

Traditional knowledge was general. What we now consider
knowledge is, of necessity, highly specialized. We never before
spoke of a man or woman 'of knowledge'. We spoke of an 'educated person'. Educated persons were generalists. They knew
enough to talk or write about a good many things, enough to
understand a good many things. But they did not know enough
to *do* any one thing. As an old saying has it: you would want an
educated person as a guest at your dinner table, but you would
not want him or her alone with you on a desert island where you
need somebody who knows how to do things. In fact, in today's
university the traditional 'educated persons' are not considered
'educated persons' at all. They are looked down upon as dilet-
tantes.

In *A Yankee at the Court of King Arthur* the hero of the 1889 book
by Mark Twain (1833-1910) was not an educated person. He
surely knew neither Latin nor Greek, had probably never read
Shakespeare and did not even know the Bible well. But he knew
how to *do* everything mechanical, up to and including generating
electricity and building telephones.

The purpose of knowledge for Socrates was self-knowledge
and self-development. Results were internal. For his antagonist,
Protagoras, the result was the ability to know what to say and to
say it well. It was 'image', to use a contemporary term. For more
than 2000 years Protagoras' concept of knowledge dominated
Western learning and defined knowledge. The medieval *trivium*,
the educational system that up to this day underlies what we call
a 'liberal education', consisted of Grammar, Logic and Rhetoric –
the tools needed to decide what to say and how to say it. They are
not tools for deciding what to *do* and how to do it. The Zen concept of knowledge and the Confucian concept of knowledge – the

two concepts that dominated Eastern learning and Eastern culture for thousands of years – were similar. The first focused on self-knowledge, the second – like the medieval *trivium* – on the Chinese equivalents of Grammar, Logic and Rhetoric.

The knowledge we *now* consider knowledge proves itself in *action*. What we now mean by knowledge is information effective in action, information focused on results. Results are *outside* the person, in society and economy, or in the advancement of knowledge itself.

To accomplish anything this knowledge has to be highly specialized. This was the reason why the tradition – beginning with the ancients but still persisting in what we call 'liberal education' – relegated it to the status of *téchne* or craft. It could neither be learned nor taught. Nor did it imply any general principle whatever. It was specific and specialized. It was experience rather than learning, training rather than schooling. But today we do not speak of these specialized knowledges as 'crafts'. We speak of 'disciplines'. This is as great a change in intellectual history as any ever recorded.

A discipline converts a 'craft' into a methodology – such as engineering, the scientific method, the quantitative method or the physician's differential diagnosis. Each of these methodologies converts *ad hoc* experience into system. Each converts anecdote into information. Each converts skill into something that can be taught and learned.

The shift from knowledge to knowledges has given knowledge the power to create a new society. But this society has to be structured on the basis of knowledge being specialized and of knowledge people being specialists. This gives them their power. But it also raises basic questions – of values, of vision, of beliefs, that is of all the things that hold society together and give meaning to life. As the last chapter of this book will discuss, it also raises a big – and a new – question: what constitutes the Educated Person in the Society of Knowledges?

2

The society of organizations

An organization is a human group, composed of specialists working together on a common task. Unlike 'society', 'community' or 'family' – the traditional social aggregates – organization is purposefully designed and grounded neither in the psychological nature of man nor in biological necessity. Yet while a human creation, it is meant to endure – not for ever perhaps but for a considerable period.

An organization is always specialized. It is defined by its task. Community and society by contrast are defined by a bond that holds together human beings, whether language, culture, history or locality. An organization is effective only if it concentrates on one task. The symphony orchestra does not attempt to cure the sick; it plays music. The hospital takes care of the sick but does not attempt to play Beethoven. A mountaineering club set up to climb Himalayan peaks does not look after the homeless in Nepal no matter how great their plight. The school concentrates on teaching and learning, the business on producing and selling goods and services, the church on converting sinners and saving souls, the law courts on settling conflicts, the military on fighting wars, the American Heart Association on research into, and prevention of, cardiac degeneration and circulatory disease. Society, community, family *are*; organizations *do*.

'Organization' has become an everyday term. Heads nod when somebody says: 'In our organization everything should revolve around the customer'; or 'All that counts in our organization is meeting the budget'; or 'In this organization they never forget a mistake you made'. Society in all developed countries has become a *society of organizations* in which most, if not all, social tasks are done in and by an organization – the business enterprise and the labour union; the armed services and the hospital; schools, and universities; a host of community services – some of them government agencies, many more (especially in the United States) non-profit institutions of the 'Social Sector' (see Chapter 9). But there are also symphony orchestras – hundreds of them in the United States – and museums and foundations and trade associations and consumer advocates, and churches, and many others.

Yet no one in the United States – or any place else – spoke of 'organizations' until after World War II. The *Concise Oxford*, England's authoritative dictionary, did not yet list the term in its current meaning in its 1950 edition. Political and social scientists speak of government and business, of society, tribe, community and family. But 'organization' still has to enter the political, economic and sociological vocabulary.

This raises three related questions:

- What functions do organizations perform? Why are they needed?
- What explains their still being ignored, by and large, in social and political science and in economics?
- Finally: What, precisely, is an 'organization'? How does it work?

The function of organization

The function of organization is to make knowledges productive. Organizations have become central to society in all developed countries because of the shift from knowledge to knowledges. The more specialized knowledges are, the more effective they will be.

The best radiologists are not the ones who know the most about medicine; they are the specialists who know how to obtain images of the body's inside through X-ray, ultrasound, body-scanner, magnetic resonance. The best market researchers are not those who know the most about business but the ones who know the most about market research.

Yet neither radiologist nor market researcher have results by themselves. Their work is 'input' only. It does not become result unless put together with the work of other specialists. Knowledges by themselves are sterile. They become productive only if welded together into knowledge. To make this possible is the task of organization, the reason for its existence, its function.

We surely overdo specialization these days – worst of all in academia. But the cure is not to try to give specialists a 'liberal education' so as to make 'generalists' out of them (as I used to advocate myself for many years). This does not work, we have learned. Specialists are effective only as specialists; and knowledge workers must be effective. The most highly effective knowledge workers do not want to be anything but narrow specialists. Neurosurgeons get better and better, the more they practise their skill. French Horn players do not take up the violin, nor should they. Specialists need exposure to the universe of knowledge (as will be further argued in Chapter 12). But they need to *work* as specialists, and to concentrate on being specialists. And for this to produce results, organization is needed.

Organization as a distinct species

But why has it taken so long for the scholars to recognize organization even though it became predominant social reality decades ago? The answer tells us a good deal about organization, and about what it is.

It is not surprising that lawyers have not concerned themselves with this new phenomenon. 'Organization' is not a legal term any more than are 'community' or 'society'. Nor is 'organization' an economic term. Some organizations pursue economic objectives, influence the economy, and are in turn influenced by it (e.g. businesses and labour unions). Many others – the Churches or the Boy Scouts – are not within the economist's purview. But why have political scientists and sociologists largely ignored a phenomenon that so profoundly affects polity and society?

There is no mention of organizations in the works of the founder of sociology, the Frenchman Auguste Comte (1798-1857). But then there were none in his time. Organization, however, also went unmentioned in the most influential non-Marxist critique of modern society, the 1888 *Gemeinschaft und Gesellschaft* (Community and Society) by the German Ferdinand Toennies (1853–1936), and in the works of the patron saints of modern sociology, the German Max Weber (1864–1920) and the Italian Vilfredo Pareto (1848–1923). All three were highly conscious of – and highly critical of – the rise of big business and big unions but quite oblivious to organizations as a new phenomenon. And it is ignored just as much in more recent social science books.

The explanation is that organization is ignored precisely *because* it profoundly affects both polity and society. Organization is incompatible with what *both* political and social scientists still assume to be 'normal'. They still assume that a normal society is unitary rather than pluralistic. But the society of organizations is profoundly pluralistic. For organization to be noticed at all by political scientist or sociologist, it has to be treated as an abnormality, and indeed a dangerous disease.

A good example is the 1924 book *The Legal Foundations of Capitalism* by the distinguished American labour economist John R. Commons (1862–1945). Commons argued that the emergence of organization in the form of the business corporation was a poison injected into the American body politic by a 'conspiracy' on the part of the late nineteenth-century Supreme Court, which wilfully misinterpreted the Fourteenth Amendment to the Constitution. That this was silly should have been obvious to any reader; every other developed country had equally accepted corporations without benefit of Supreme Court or Fourteenth Amendment – indeed the United States was the last of all developed countries to do so (later even than Japan). Yet Commons made sense to the reader of 1924. Organization was such an aberration that it could only be explained by some sinister conspiracy. The book became a bestseller and one of the 'bibles' of the New Deal 'business bashers' a few years later.

The emergence of organization has been a 'paradigm shift', to use the term coined by the American philosopher Thomas Kuhn (born 1922) in his 1962 book *The Structure of Scientific Revolutions*. It contradicted what political and social scientists *know* to be reality. And then, as Kuhn pointed out, it takes between 30 and 50 years – that is, until a new generation has grown up and taken over – before the new reality is seen, let alone accepted, by the scholarly community.

There is another reason still why so little attention has so far been paid to organizations. Armies, churches, universities, hospitals, businesses, labour unions have been seen, studied, analysed for a long time and in great detail. But each of them has been treated as unique, as being *sui generis*. Even now interviewers are surprised when I tell them that my consulting practice has included all these institutions for more than 40 years. Only very recently has it been realized that all belong to the same species; they are all 'organizations'. They are the man-made environment, the 'social ecology' of post-capitalist society. They have far more in common with one another than they differ. As said earlier, most people – and practically everybody outside the United States – still hear 'business' when they hear 'management' and do not yet realize that management is a *generic* function pertaining to all organizations alike.* Only the emergence of management since World War II has made us see that organization is something distinct and discrete. It is neither 'community' nor 'society' nor 'class' nor 'family', the modern integrators which social scientists know. But it is also not 'clan' or 'tribe' or 'kinship group' or any of the other integrators of traditional society known and studied by anthropologists, ethnographers and sociologists. Organization is something new and distinct – *but what is it*?

The characteristics of organization

Organizations are special-purpose institutions. They are effective because they concentrate on *one task*.

If you were to go to the American Lung Association and say: '90% of all adult Americans (it's always 90% by the way) suffer from ingrown toe nails; we need your expertise in research, health education and prevention to stamp out this dreadful scourge', you'd surely get the answer: 'We are interested only in what lies

---

* As pointed out in my 1990 book *Managing the Non-Profit Organization*, a good many people in the non-profit sector still see churches as churches, hospitals as hospitals, community services as community services, rather than seeing all of them as belonging to the same family, the non-profits, and the same species, the organization.

between the hips and the shoulders and even there in only part of the anatomy.'

This explains why the American Lung Association or the American Heart Association or any of the others in the health field have results. Society, community, family have to deal with whatever problem arises. To do so in an organization is 'diversification'. And in an organization diversification is splintering. It destroys the performance capacity of an organization whether a business, a union, a school, a hospital, a community service, a church. Organization is a *tool*. As with any tool, the more specialized, the greater its performance capacity for its given task.

Because the organization is composed of specialists, each with his or her own narrow knowledge area, its *mission* must be crystal clear. The organization must be single-minded. Otherwise its members become confused. They will follow their specialty rather than apply it to the common task. They will each define 'results' in terms of their specialty. They will each impose their own values on the organization. Only a clear, focused and common mission can hold the organization together and enable it to produce results. And without a clear, focused mission the organization soon loses credibility.

A good example is what happened to American Protestantism in the post-World War II period as a result of 'Social Christianity'. Very few strategies have ever been as successful as that of the American Protestant churches, when around 1900 they focused their tremendous resources on the social needs of a rapidly industrializing urban society. Social Christianity was a major reason why the churches in America did not become marginal, as the churches in Europe did. Yet social action is not the mission of a Christian church. It is to save souls. Because Social Christianity was so successful, the churches, especially since World War II, dedicated themselves, however, more and more to 'social causes'. Ultimately, Liberal Protestantism used the trappings of Christianity to further social reform and to promote social legislation. Churches became social agencies. They became politicized – and they rapidly lost cohesion, appeal and members.

The prototype of the modern organization is the symphony orchestra. Each of the 250 musicians in the orchestra is a specialist, and a high-grade one to boot. Yet by itself the tuba doesn't make music; only the orchestra does. The orchestra performs only because all 250 musicians have the same score. They all subordinate their specialty to a common task. And they all play only one piece of music at any given time.

Results in an organization are always on the outside. Society, community, family are self-contained and self-sufficient. They exist for their own sake. But all organizations exist to produce results on the outside.

Inside a business there are only costs. 'Profit centre' (a term which, alas, I myself coined many years ago) is a misnomer. Inside a business there are only *cost* centres. There are profits only when a customer has bought the product or the service and has paid for it. The result of the hospital is a cured patient who can go back home (and who fervently hopes never to have to come back to the hospital). The results of the school or the university are graduates who put to work what they have learned in their own life and work. The results of an army are not manoeuvres and promotions for generals; they are deterring a war or winning it. The results of the church are not even on this earth.

This means that results in an organization are always pretty far away from what each member contributes. This is true even in the hospital where individual contributions – that of the nurse or the physical therapist – are closely related to the result: a cured patient. But many specialists, even in the hospital, cannot identify their contribution to any particular result. What share in the recovery or rehabilitation of a patient does the X-ray technician have? Or the clinical laboratory? Or the dietician?

In most institutions the individual's contribution is totally swallowed up in the task and disappears in it. In the symphony orchestra only the organization has results. What use is the best engineering department if the company goes bankrupt? And yet unless the engineering department is first-class, dedicated and hard working, the company is likely to go bankrupt. Each member in an organization, in other words, makes (at least in theory) a vital contribution without which there are no results. But none by himself or herself produces these results.

This then requires, as an absolute prerequisite of an organization's performance, that task and mission be crystal clear. Results need to be defined clearly and unambiguously – and, if at all possible, measurably.

This also requires that an organization appraise and judge itself and its performance against clear, known, impersonal objectives and goals. Neither society nor community nor family have to do this or could do this. Survival rather than performance is their test.

Joining an organization is always a decision. *De facto* there may be little choice. But even where membership is all but compulsory – as membership in the Christian Church was in all countries of Europe for many centuries for all but a handful of Jews and gypsies – the fiction of a decision to join is carefully maintained. The godfather at the infant's baptism pledges the child's *voluntary* acceptance of membership in the Church.

It may be difficult to leave an organization – the Mafia, for instance, a big Japanese company, the Jesuit Order. But it is always possible. And the more an organization becomes an organization of knowledge workers, the easier it is to leave it and move elsewhere (as will be further discussed in the section on the 'Employee Society' later in this chapter).

Unlike society, community and family, an organization is therefore always in competition for its most essential resource: qualified, knowledgeable, dedicated people.

This means that organizations have to market membership, whether as employee, as volunteer or as communicant, fully as much as they market their products and services – and perhaps more. They have to attract people, have to hold people, have to recognize and reward people, have to motivate people, have to serve and satisfy people.

Because modern organization is an organization of knowledge specialists it has to be an organization of equals, of 'colleagues' of 'associates'. No knowledge 'ranks' higher than another. The position of each is determined by its contribution to the common task rather than by any inherent superiority or inferiority. 'Philosophy is the Queen of the Sciences' says an old tag. But to remove a kidney stone you want a urologist rather than a logician. The modern organization cannot be an organization of 'boss' and 'subordinate'. It must be organized as a team of 'associates'.

An organization is always *managed*. Society, community, family may have 'leaders – and so do organizations. But organizations, and organizations alone, are managed. The managing may be perfunctory and intermittent – as it is, for instance, in the Parent-Teachers Association at a suburban school in the United States where the elected officers spend only a few hours each year on the organization's affairs. Or management may be a full-time and demanding job for a fairly large group of people, as in the military, the business enterprise, the union, the university and many others. But there have to be people who make decisions, or nothing will ever get done. There have to be people who are accountable for the organization's mission, its spirit, its performance, its results. There must be a 'conductor' who controls the 'score'. There have to be people who focus the organization on its mission, set the strategy to carry it out and define what the results are. This management has to have considerable authority. But its job in the knowledge organization is not to command. It is to direct.

Finally, to be able to perform, an organization must be autonomous. Legally it may be a government agency, as are Europe's universities, America's state universities or Europe's hospitals. Yet in actual operation these organizations must be able to 'do their thing'. If they are used to carry out 'government policy' they immediately stop performing.

All this, it will be said, is obvious. Yet every one of these characteristics are new, and is indeed unique to that new social phenomenon, the organization.

Organization as a destabilizer

Society, community, family are all conserving institutions. They try to maintain stability and to prevent, or at least to slow, change. But the organization of the post-capitalist society of organizations is a *destabilizer*. Because its function is to put knowledge to work – on tools, processes and products; on work; on knowledge itself – it must be organized for constant change. It must be organized for innovation – and innovation as the Austro-American economist Joseph Schumpeter (1883–1950) said, is 'creative destruction'. It must be organized for systematic abandonment of the established, the customary, the familiar, the comfortable, whether products, services and processes, human and social relationships, skills or organizations themselves. It is of the nature of knowledge that it changes fast and that today's certainties become tomorrow's absurdities.

Skills, in contrast to knowledge, change slowly and infrequently. If Socrates, the stonemason, came back to life today and

went to work in a stonemason's yard the only change of
significance would be that he had to turn out tombstones with a
cross on them instead of steles with the symbol of Hermes. The
tools are the same. Only now they have electric batteries in the
handles.* For 400 years after Gutenberg first used movable type
there was practically no change in the craft of printing – until the
steam engine came in, that is, until the discipline of engineering
was being applied to a *téchne*. Throughout history craftspeople
who had learned a trade had learned everything they would ever
have to use during their lifetime after five or six years of apprenticeship at age 17 or 18. In the post-capitalist society it is safe to
assume that anyone with any knowledge will have to acquire *new*
knowledge every four or five years, or else become obsolete.

The changes that most profoundly affect a knowledge do not,
as a rule, come out of its own area – as the example of printing
shows. The pharmaceutical industry is being profoundly changed
today by knowledge that comes out of genetics and biology, disciplines of which few people in a pharmaceutical laboratory had
even heard of 40 years ago. The greatest challenge to the railways
came not from changes in railways but from the car, the lorry and
the aircraft.

Social innovation is as important as new science or new technology in creating new knowledge and in making old ones obsolete. Indeed social innovation is often more important. What
triggered the present worldwide crisis of that proudest of nineteenth-century institutions, the commercial bank, was not the
computer or any other technological change. It was the realization
that an old but hitherto rather obscure financial instrument, commercial paper, could be used by non-banks to finance companies.
This speedily deprived the banks of the business on which they
had a monopoly for 200 years and which gave them most of their
income: the commercial loan. The greatest change most probably
is that in the last 40 years *purposeful innovation* – both technical
and social – has itself become an organized discipline which is
both teachable and learnable.†

---

* A small museum on the Spanish Costa Brava near the ancient city of
Emporia exhibits the tools the craftsmen of the second and third centuries AD
used. No craftsman today would have the slightest difficulty figuring out how to
use them. He would hardly notice that the tools are 2000 years old.

† On this, see my 1985 book *Innovation and Entrepreneurship* (London:
Heinemann).

Nor is rapid knowledge-based change confined to business as is still widely believed. It clearly is needed if the labour union – another of the 'success stories' of capitalist society – is to survive. No organization in the 50 years since World War II has changed more than the military, even though uniforms and titles of rank have remained the same. Weapons changed completely, as the Iraq War of 1991 dramatically demonstrated. Military doctrines and concepts have changed even more drastically. And so have organization structures, command structures, relationships and responsibilities.

One implication: every organization of today has to build into its very structure the *management of change*.

It has to build in organized abandonment of everything it does. It has to learn to ask every few years of every process, every product, every procedure, every policy: 'If we did not do this already, would we go into it now knowing what we now know?' And if the answer is 'no' the organization has to ask: 'And what do we *do* now?' It has to *do* something and not just make another study. Indeed, organizations increasingly will have to *plan* abandonment rather than try to prolong, as long as possible, the life of a successful policy, practice or product – something which so far only a few large Japanese companies have faced up to.*

But *creating the new* also has to be built into the organization. Specifically, every organization has to build into its very fabric three systematic practices. It first needs continuing improvement of everything it does – the process the Japanese call *kaizen*. Every artist throughout history has practised *kaizen*, that is, organized, continuous self-improvement. But only the Japanese so far – perhaps because of their Zen tradition – have embodied it in the daily life and work of the business organization (although not into their singularly change-resistant universities). The aim of *kaizen* is to improve product or service so that it becomes a truly different product or service in two or three years' time.

Every organization will, second, have to learn to *exploit*, that is, to develop new applications from its own successes. Again Japanese businesses have done their best job in this so far, as witness how the Japanese consumer electronics manufacturers have developed one new product after another out of the same

* On this see Chapter 24, 'The New Japanese Business Strategies', in my 1992 book *Managing for the Future* (Oxford: Butterworth-Heinemann).

American invention, the tape recorder. But building on their successes is also one of the strengths of the American 'pastoral' churches whose fast growth is beginning to offset the steady decline of both the traditional 'Social Christianity' and Fundamentalist churches.

Every organization finally will have to learn to innovate – and innovation can be organized as a systematic process and should be organized as such.

And then, of course, one comes back to abandonment and the process starts all over again.

Unless this is done the knowledge-based post-capitalist organization will very soon find itself obsolescent, will soon find itself losing performance capacity and with it the ability to attract and to hold the knowledge specialists on whom it depends.

Another implication – post-capitalist society has to be decentralized. Its organizations must be able to make fast decisions, be based on closeness to performance, closeness to the market, closeness to technology, closeness to the changes in society, environment, demographics, knowledge, which must be seen and utilized as opportunities for innovation.

Organizations of the post-capitalist society thus constantly upset, disorganize, destabilize the community. They must change the demand for skills and knowledges. Just when every technical university is geared up to teach physics, geneticists are what we need. Just when the banks have organized credit analysis they need investment people. Businesses close factories on which local communities depend for employment, or replace grizzled model makers who have spent years learning their craft, with 25-year-old 'whiz kids' who know computer simulation. Hospitals move the delivery of babies into a free-standing 'birthing centre' when the knowledge base and technology of obstetrics change. We must be able to close a hospital altogether when changes in medical knowledge, practice and technology make a hospital with fewer than 200 beds uneconomical and incapable of giving first-rate care. Similarly, for the school or the college to discharge its social function we must be able to close down a school or a college – no matter how deeply rooted in the local community and how much loved by it – if changes in demographics, technology or knowledge make a different size or a different philosophy a prerequisite of performance.

But every one of such changes upsets the community, disrupts it, deprives it of continuity. Every one is 'unfair'. Every one destabilizes.

Modern organization creates yet another tension for the community. It must operate in a community. Its members live in that community, speak its language, send their children to its schools, vote in it, pay taxes to it. They have to be at home in it. Their results are in the community. Yet the organization cannot submerge itself into the community or subordinate itself to it. Its 'culture' has to transcend community.

As the American anthropologist Edward T. Hall (born 1914) pointed out in his 1959 book *The Silent Language,* important communications in every society are not verbal but cultural – through the way people stand, the way they move, the way they act. Hall pointed out that a German physician uses quite different signals to get a message across to a German patient from the signals the English, American or Japanese physician uses. American civil servants would be completely baffled in their own Washington if they were to sit in on the meeting of the local grocery chain that discusses next week's advertising promotion. But they easily understand what a Chinese colleague tells them about bureaucratic intrigues in Beijing. And, despite all we hear about differences in 'management style', a large Japanese company functions very much like a large American, a large German or a large British company.

The nature of the task determines the culture of an organization rather than the community in which the task is being performed. Each organization's value system is determined by its task. Every hospital in the world, every school in the world, every business in the world has to believe that what it is doing is the essential contribution to its community and society – the contribution on which all the others in the community depend in the last analysis. To perform its task it has to be organized and managed the same way. In its culture the organization thus always transcends the community. If an organization's culture clashes with the values of its community, the organization's culture will prevail – or else the organization will not make its social contribution.

'Knowledge knows no boundaries' says an old proverb. There are as yet very few 'transnational' organizations and not even a great many 'multinationals'. But *every* knowledge organization is, of necessity, non-national, non-community. Even if totally embedded in the local community, it is a 'rootless cosmopolitan', to use one of Hitler's and Stalin's favourite epithets.

The employee society

Only 50 years ago 'employee' was rarely used in English or American, except as a legal term. People then spoke of 'capital and labour' or of 'management and the worker'. The German equivalent, *Mitarbeiter*, was then equally uncommon. And when the term was used, it meant low-level clerical people – the equivalent to the Spanish *empleado* or the German *Angestellter*. 'Employee' is also an awkward word. It has no clear meaning. And all equivalents for the word in other languages are equally recent in common usage and equally awkward. The phenomenon itself is new – and we have no proper word for it as yet.

An 'employee' is, by definition, somebody who gets paid for working. Yet in the United States the largest single group of 'employees' are people who work without pay. Every second adult American – 90 million people altogether – works as an unpaid employee for a non-profit organization, most of them giving at least three hours a week of unpaid work.* They are clearly 'staff' and consider themselves as such. Yet they are volunteers and receive no pay.

Many people who, in effect, work as 'employees' are not employed in any legal sense. They are 'self-employed'. A century ago people who were employed, that is, worked for somebody else, worked for a 'master' rather than for an organization or a 'boss'. There were the factory workers; there were the domestic servants – until World War I vastly outnumbering factory workers in every developed country. There were shop assistants, sales people, and so on. People with education worked as 'independents' by and large. And the largest single group in the 1913 workforce in any country (except Britain and Belgium) were farmers working for themselves on land they either owned or rented.

Today farmers are a tiny minority in every developed country. Domestic servants have all but disappeared. But the people who 60 or 70 years ago were 'independent' are now employees or 'self-employed', that is, the people of education and knowledge.

We need a word to describe these people – and we do not have one. In the meantime we may have to do with defining 'employees' in the post-capitalist society as people whose ability to make

* On this, see Chapter 9.

a contribution depends on their having access to an organization. Whether they are paid is secondary. If these people are 'self-employed' they function because they render services to or through organizations: physicians under the British National Health Service; their American counterparts working for an 'Independent Providers' group; accountants and auditors. These people may not receive a 'wage'. They receive a 'fee'. But their ability to function depends fully as much on their access to an organization as if they were on the payroll.

The higher up we go in terms of income, education or social status, the more does ability to perform and function depend on access to the organization. Just as post-capitalist society has become a society of organizations, it has become a society of employees. These are only two different ways to describe the same phenomenon.

As far as the employees are concerned who work in subordinate and menial service occupations – the check-out assistant in the supermarket; the cleaner in the hospital; the driver of the delivery truck – their position may not be too different from that of the wage earner, the 'worker' of yesterday, whose direct descendants they are. They account for a quarter or more of the workforce; they already outnumber industrial workers. Their position, their pro-ductivity; their dignity are central social problems of the post-capi-talist society (as will be discussed in Chapter 4).

But the position of the next group, the knowledge workers, is radically different.

All knowledge workers can work only because there is an orga-nization. In that respect they are dependent. But at the same time they own the 'means of production', that is, their knowledge. And knowledge workers account for a third or more of the total work-force of a developed country (with skilled service workers accounting for another third or so).

Marx believed that the greatest change in society resulting from the introduction of capitalism was the 'alienation' of the worker. Workers no longer owned the tools of production. They could produce only if somebody else, that is, the 'capitalists', furnished the tools, especially the steadily more expensive machinery.

The knowledge employee still needs the tools. The capital investment in the tools of the knowledge employee may already he higher than the capital investment in the tools of the manufac-turing worker ever was (and the social investment, e.g. in the

knowledge worker's education, is, of course, many times the
investment in the manual worker's education). But this capital
investment is unproductive unless the knowledge employees
bring to bear on it the knowledge which they own and which
cannot be taken away from them.

Machine operators in the factory did as they were told. The
machine decided not only what to do but how to do it. The
knowledge employee may need a machine whether it be a computer, an ultrasound analyser of a patient's prostate or the
astronomer's telescope. But neither the computer nor the ultrasound analyser nor the telescope tell the knowledge employee
what to do, let alone how to do it. Without this knowledge, which
is the property of the employee, the machine is unproductive.

The worker under capitalism was totally dependent on the
machine. In the employee society the employee and the tools of
production are interdependent. One without the other cannot
function. And while the tools of production, e.g. the ultrasound
analyser, are fixed in place, the technician who knows how to
run them and how to interpret their readings has mobility. The
machine is dependent on the employee, not the other way
round.

Workers throughout history could be 'supervised'. They could
be told what to do, how to do it, how fast to do it, and so on.
Knowledge employees cannot, in effect, be supervised. Unless
they know more than anybody else in the organization, they are
useless to all intents and purposes.

The marketing manager may tell the market researcher what
the company needs to know about the design of a new product
and the market segment in which it should be positioned. But it
is the market researcher's job to tell the president of the company what market research is needed, how to set it up and what
the results mean. The commander of an airbase decides how
many planes and of what kind are needed for a certain mission.
But it is the crew chief, though vastly inferior in rank (and usually not even a commissioned officer), who tells the commander
how many planes are airworthy and what repairs they need
before they can be sent off on their mission. It is a very foolish
commander who overrules his crew chief despite all the difference in rank – and a commander, by the way, who will not last
very long.

Employees in the employee society need access to an organization. Without it they cannot produce or perform. And yet they have mobility. They carry the means of production, their knowledge, with them.

In the 1980s and 1990s during the traumatic restructuring of American business, thousands (if not hundreds of thousands) of knowledge employees lost their jobs. Their companies were acquired, merged, spun off, liquidated and so on. Yet within a very few months, the great majority found new jobs in which to put their knowledge to work. The transition period was painful. And in about half the cases the new jobs did not pay quite as much as the old ones and may not have been as enjoyable. But laid-off technicians, professionals and managers found that they had the 'capital' – their knowledge; they owned the *means* of production. Somebody else, the organization, had the *tools* of production. The two needed each other. By itself neither was capable of producing. Neither, in other words, is 'dependent' or 'independent'. They are interdependent.

Japan officially still believes in lifetime commitment, and especially for knowledge employees, for professionals, for managers, for technicians. But the great scandal of Japan in 1989 was the 'Recruit Affair', in which a rapidly growing publisher, Recruit, bribed politicians by giving them shares for free. What made these Recruit shares so attractive? What made Recruit so extraordinarily profitable? The company publishes magazines for technicians, professionals and middle managers who look for better jobs than they presently have. These magazines contain nothing but job offers for such people. When riding on the Tokyo subway, the foreigner is told, older people read adult comics; but younger people read the magazines which offer positions for knowledge employees already employed by other companies. Even in Japan the knowledge employee is rapidly gaining mobility despite all the emphasis on 'loyalty' and 'lifetime commitment'.

'Loyalty' from now on cannot be obtained by the paycheque. It has to be earned by proving to knowledge employees that the organization which presently employs them offers them exceptional opportunities for being effective and performing. Not so long ago we talked about 'labour'; increasingly we are talking of 'human resources'. This implies, especially in regard to people of knowledge, that it is the individual knowledge employee who decides in large measure what he or she contributes, and how great the yield from his or her knowledge can or should be.

But in the knowledge society even low-skilled service workers are not 'proletarians'. The employees collectively *own* the means of production. Individually few of them are wealthy. Even fewer of them are rich (though a good many are financially independent – what we now call 'affluent'). Collectively, however, whether through their pension funds, through mutual funds, through their retirement accounts and so on, they own the means of production. The people who exercise the voting power for the employees are themselves employees, e.g. the civil servants who manage the pension funds of states and local governments in the United States. These pension-fund managers are the only true 'capitalists' in the United States. The 'capitalists' have thus themselves become employees in the post-capitalist knowledge society. They are paid as employees. They think as employees. They see themselves as employees. But they act as capitalists.

One implication is that capital now serves the employee where under Capitalism the employee served capital. But another implication is that we will have to rethink and to redefine the role, power and function of capital and ownership. As will be discussed (in Chapter 3), we have to rethink the *governance of corporations*.

3

Labour, capital and their future

If knowledge is *the* resource of post-capitalist society, what then will be the future role and function of the two key resources of capitalist (and of socialist) society; labour and capital?

Socially the *new* challenges – to be discussed in Chapters 4 and 5 and in this book's last part – will dominate. On our answers to them the success of post-capitalist society will largely depend. But *politically* the unfinished business of capitalist society will be highly visible: the disappearance of labour as a factor of production, and the redefinition of the role and function of traditional capital.

We have moved already into an 'employee society' where labour no longer is an asset. We equally have moved into a 'capitalism' without capitalists – which defies everything still considered self-evident truths, if not 'laws of nature' – by politicians, lawyers, economists, journalists, union leaders, business leaders; in short, by almost everybody, regardless of political persuasion. For that reason, these issues will be in the *political* spotlight in the decades ahead. To be able to tackle successfully the *new* challenges of this transition period we must first resolve these two items of 'unfinished business': the future role and function of labour and the future role and function of money-capital.

Is labour still an asset?

American manufacturing production remained almost unchanged as a percentage of GNP in the years of the 'manufacturing decline'. It stood at 22% of GNP in 1975 and 23% in 1990. During those 20 years GNP increased two and a half times. In other words, total American manufacturing production grew *more* than two and a half times in these 20 years.

But manufacturing employment did not increase at all. On the contrary, it went down from 1960 to 1990 as a percentage of the workforce and even in absolute numbers. It fell by almost half in these 30 years, from 25% of the total workforce in 1960 to 16% or 17% in 1990. During this time the total American workforce doubled – the largest increase ever recorded by any country in peacetime. All the increase was, however, in jobs other than in making and moving things.

These trends are certain to continue. Unless there is a severe depression, manufacturing production in America is likely to stay at about the same 23% of GNP, which, for the next 10 or 15 years, should mean another near-doubling. During the same period, however, employment in manufacturing is likely to fall to 12% or less of the total workforce. This would mean a further fairly sharp shrinkage of the total number of people employed in manufacturing work.

The development in Japan is almost exactly the same. There, too, total manufacturing production has increased two and a half times in the 20 years between 1970 and 1990. There, too, however, manufacturing employment in total numbers has not increased at all. And there, too, from now on even a sizable increase in manufacturing production will not be sufficient to offset the steady shrinkage in manufacturing jobs. In Japan, too, by the year 2000 total employment in manufacturing will be substantially less than it was in 1990.

The response of these two countries to identical developments is, however, completely different. In the United States there is gloom about the 'decline of American manufacturing', if not panic about the 'death of American manufacturing'. In the United

States manufacturing is equated with blue-collar *employment*. In Japan the reaction has been the opposite. What matters to the Japanese is the increase in manufacturing *production*. Japan sees the trends of the last 20 years as victory. America sees them as defeat. Japan sees the glass as 'half-full', America as 'half-empty'.

As a result of these differences in attitude the policies of the two countries are also radically different. Every state, county and city in America is desperately trying to attract manufacturers who offer blue-collar jobs. Poor rural states like Kentucky and Tennessee have lured Japanese car manufacturers with offers of long-range tax benefits and low-interest loans. The city of Los Angeles in early 1992 awarded a multi-*billion* dollar contract for rapid-transit equipment to the company that promised to create all of 97 manufacturing jobs in a region that has almost 15 million inhabitants!

By contrast, Japanese companies are moving manual work in manufacturing out of Japan as fast as they can – into the United States; into plants at the US-Mexican border; into Indonesia.

In the United States manufacturing jobs are seen as a priceless asset. In Japan they are more and more seen as a liability.

Differences in social structure between the two countries explain, in part, these different reactions to the same trends. The shrinkage of manual jobs in making and moving things is, above all, a threat to America's most visible minority, the Blacks. Their biggest economic gains in the last 30 years came from moving into well-paid jobs in unionized mass-production industries. In all other areas of economy and society Black gains have been much more modest. The shrinkage of jobs in the unionized mass-production industries therefore aggravates what all along has been America's most serious problem – all the more daunting as it is as much a problem of conscience as it is a social problem.

In Japan practically all young people now get a high-school degree – and then are considered over-qualified for manual work. They become clerical workers. Those who go on to university – and the same proportion of young males goes to university in Japan as in the United States – take managerial or professional jobs only. If Japan were not able to cut the number of manual jobs in manufacturing it would face an extreme labour shortage. In other words, the shrinkage in manufacturing jobs is the answer to a problem for the Japanese.

A country needs a manufacturing base, Americans would

argue – and most Europeans as well. This means manufacturing jobs. But, the Japanese argue – and convincingly – that the supply of young people in the developing countries qualified for nothing but manual work in manufacturing is so large – and will remain so large for at least another 30 years – that worrying about the 'industrial base' is nonsense. A country that has the knowledge workers to design products and to market them will have no difficulty getting these products made at low cost and high quality. In fact, the Japanese argue that to encourage blue-collar manual work in making and moving things *weakens* a developed economy. In a developed economy even people who learn little in school represent a tremendous educational investment. If employed as manufacturing workers even such people yield only a pitiful return to society and economy, perhaps no more than 1% or 2%. Yet people in developing countries who have had no schooling are fully as productive after a little training as any manual worker in the most highly developed country. Economically as well as socially it would be much more productive – the Japanese argue – to put the money spent to create blue-collar jobs in developed countries instead into advancing the country's education and thus ensure that youngsters learn enough to become qualified for knowledge work or at least for high-level service work.

How much labour is needed and what kind?

A developed country does indeed need a manufacturing base. Yet the facts support the Japanese position. The United States still has the world's strongest agricultural base even though farmers are now only 3% of the working population (they still were 25% at the end of World War II). The United States equally could still be the world's largest manufacturer with manufacturing workers constituting no more than 10% – or less – of the working population.

In 1980 United States Steel, America's largest integrated steel company, employed 120 000 people. Ten years later it employed 20 000 people, and yet produced almost the same steel tonnage. Within 10 years the productivity of the manual worker engaged in steel making had increased sevenfold. A large part of the increase was obtained by closing down old, outmoded plants. A large part came from investment in new equipment. But the lion's share of the jump in productivity represents re-engineering work flow and tasks.

As a result, United States Steel's best mills are now the world's most productive *integrated* steel makers. And yet they – and all integrated steel mills the world over – are still grossly over-staffed. And America's integrated steel mills are still losing money. 'Minimills' – and in 1991 almost one-third of all steel pro-duced in the United States was produced by minimills – are again three to four times as productive as the most productive inte-grated mill. The best of American minimills could probably pro-duce as much steel as United States Steel with not much more than one-sixth of the latter's present employment. And increas-ingly the minimills can turn out all the products an integrated steel mill produces and of the same or better quality.

To be sure, a minimill obtains these results by not having to perform the most labour-intensive operations of an integrated steel mill. It does not smelt iron ore to obtain iron. Nor does it convert iron into steel. It starts with scrap steel. But for the fore-seeable future, the world will have abundant supplies of scrap steel.

But the process is not the main difference between the inte-grated steel mill and the minimill. Workers in the minimill are not blue-collar workers making and moving things. They are knowl-edge workers. The minimill changes steel making from applying muscle and skill to work to applying knowledge to work: knowl-edge of the process; of chemistry; of metallurgy; of computer operations. The workers whom United States Steel laid off need not apply at the minimill.

This is an extreme example to be sure. But it indicates the direc-tion. Plenty of people will always be needed who can bring only muscle to the job. With our present knowledge of training they can quickly be made productive in traditional jobs. Even more people will be needed who can bring only manual skills to the job. But the greatest employment need of the next decades will be for 'technicians'. Technicians not only need high skill. They also need a high degree of formal knowledge and, above all, high capacity to learn and to acquire additional knowledge. Technicians are not the successors to yesterday's blue-collar worker. They are basically the successors to yesterday's highly skilled workers – or rather they are highly skilled workers who now also possess a substantial amount of formal knowledge, formal education and capacity for continuous learning.

A hot dispute now rages in academia and among policy makers. Is it enough of a 'manufacturing base' for developed countries to have their businesses carry on at home the work on technology, design and marketing of industrial products? Or do they also have to manufacture at home? The question is moot. If a country has the knowledge base it will also manufacture. But this manufacturing work will not be competitive if carried out by traditional blue-collar workers who serve the machine. In competitive manufacturing the work will largely be done by knowledge workers whom the machine serves – as computer consoles and computerized workstations serve the 97 technicians in a steel-making minimill.

This will create tremendous problems for *developing* countries. They can no longer expect to be able to obtain large numbers of manufacturing jobs by training low-wage people. Manual labour, no matter how cheap, will not be able to compete with knowledge labour, no matter how well paid. But this also creates tremendous problems for countries – the United States is the prime example – in which there are large groups of 'minority' people who are 'developing' rather than 'developed' in their educational qualifications. The United Kingdom, in its old working-class enclaves in the north, in Scotland especially along the Clyde, and in Northern Ireland faces a similar problem of a working-class culture which, in effect, is a culture of a developing country rather than of a developed country. On the continent of Europe, too, despite an educational system with relatively open access, the trend towards labour becoming a liability rather than an asset will, for a fairly long transition period, create both serious social problems and political conflicts. Everywhere it also raises difficult and highly emotional questions regarding the role, function and future of this century's most successful organization, the union.

To maintain and strengthen the country's manufacturing base and to ensure its remaining competitive surely deserves high priority. But this means accepting that manual labour in making and moving things is rapidly becoming a liability rather than an asset. Knowledge has become the key resource for all work. Creating traditional manufacturing jobs – as the Americans, the British and the Europeans are doing – is, at best, a short-lived expedient. It may actually make things worse. The only long-time policy which promises success is for developed countries to convert manufacturing from being labour-based into being knowledge-based.

Capitalism without capitalists

Never before have there been such enormous pools of money as are now held in developed countries by institutional investors, primarily pension funds. In the United States, where the development started and has gone the furthest, the biggest pension fund holds assets of $80 billion. And even a small pension fund may have something like $1 billion invested in the economy. These pools of capital dwarf anything the greatest 'capitalist' of past times commanded. The age structure of a developed society virtually guarantees that the pension funds will become even more important in every single developed country.

This is an unprecedented development.* It only began in the 1950s. It is so new, in fact, that the management and regulation of the pension funds are still to be worked out.

How to protect such enormous pools of money against looters is one big problem. In the United States the pension funds of private businesses have some protection against being looted. It would not have been easy in the United States to loot pension funds the way Robert Maxwell, the late British newspaper magnate, did in 1990 and 1991. But even in the United States the safeguards are woefully inadequate. No safeguards at all exist, even in the United States, against the most serious danger: the looting for political purposes of the pension funds of government employees.

In fact, in the United States the pension funds of public employees, whether those of New York City, of New York State, of Philadelphia, of the State of California and so on, have regularly been misused to plug holes in the budgets of states and cities.

And equally great is the danger that special-interest groups, e.g. labour unions, will use their political power to divert pension fund money to subsidize themselves – usually under the fraudulent pretext of making pension fund money serve 'socially

* It was first seen and analysed in my 1976 book, *The Unseen Revolution*, soon to be republished by Transaction Publishers, New Brunswick, NJ, under the title *The Pension Fund Revolution*.

constructive purposes'. Pension funds are the savings of today's employees. They must not serve anything or anyone except the financial future of the present employees. This is the greatest 'social purpose' they can possibly serve.

The pension fund and its owners

To integrate the pension funds 'real owners', present employees and future pensioners into the management of the pension fund is a challenge so far not tackled in any country. At present the only relationship these owners have is their expectation of a cheque in the future. Yet for most people over 45 in developed countries the stake in the pension fund is their largest single asset.

In the nineteenth century the biggest financial need of common people was for life insurance to protect their families in the event of their early death. With life expectancies almost double those of the nineteenth century the biggest need of common people is protection against the threat of living too long. The nineteenth century 'life insurance' was really 'death insurance'. The pension fund is 'old-age' insurance. It is an essential institution in a society in which most people can expect to outlive their working life by many years.

The regulation of pension funds and their protection against looting will remain a challenge to policy makers and law makers for years to come. In all likelihood, the challenge will only be met after we have had a few nasty scandals. Similarly, the integration of the real owners into the pension fund structure will require years of debate, of experimentation, of 'scandals'.

The proper management of the pension funds and their integrity will also be major public issues – and deservedly so. But these issues do not primarily concern us in this book. Our concern is with the *role and function of capital* now that institutional investors, and especially the pension funds, are rapidly becoming the major sources of capital in developed countries. In the United States by the end of 1992 institutional investors held at least 50% of the share capital of large corporations. They also held an almost equal proportion of the fixed debt even of America's medium-sized – let alone America's large – businesses, whether publicly or privately owned. And the one hundred largest pension funds in the United

States held something like one-third of all pension funds assets by the end of 1992.

No such concentration of financial control ever existed in the United States before – in fact it would never have been allowed.

Historically, the United States always had the lowest concentration of financial power. In Germany, for at least a century, a very few large banks have controlled – directly and through shares held by them for their customers – something like three-fifths of the voting power in Germany's large and even medium-sized companies. In Japan the *keiretsu*, the groups formed around a bank or a trading company such as Mitsubishi, Mitsui or Sumitomo, have traditionally controlled the majority of Japan's large businesses. Italy similarly has an extremely high concentration in which financial power and control is shared, partly in competition and partly in cooperation, between a very small number of highly concentrated private groups and an equally small number of government consortia controlled by and beholden to political parties.

For the United States, however, the concentration of capital in the institutional investors is unprecedented. Yet it is the US development that is likely to become the model.

The traditional way in which financial power was concentrated in Japan and Europe will not survive the rise of the pension fund. And the traditional institutions in which financial power has been concentrated in Japan, in Germany, in France, in Italy are most unlikely to be able to extend their control to the new pension funds. Different countries will undoubtedly structure the pension-fund economy their own way, just as they structured their own way the 'finance capitalism' which emerged in the closing years of the nineteenth century. But pension-fund capitalism (or pension-fund socialism for ownership of the means of production by the employees, that is, through their pension funds, is technically 'socialism' rather than 'capitalism') will become the universal ownership mode in developed countries – the age structure of developed countries alone makes this practically inevitable.

But pension-fund capitalism is fundamentally as different from any earlier form of capitalism, as it is different from anything any socialist ever envisaged as a socialist economy.

Pension funds are a curious and indeed paradoxical phenomenon. They are 'investors' who control huge pools of capital and its investment. But neither the managers who run them nor their owners are 'capitalists'. Pension-fund capitalism is capitalism *sans* capitalists.

Legally, pension funds are 'owners'; but only legally. In the first place, the pension funds are 'trustees'. The owners are the ultimate beneficiaries, that is, the future pensioners. And the pension funds are themselves managed by employees such as financial analysts, portfolio managers, actuaries. These are well-paid professionals, but unlikely to be rich themselves. Indeed, the largest of the American pension funds – the pension funds of the employees of the federal government, of the states and of the cities – are managed by civil servants who are being paid as such.

Pension-fund capitalism is also capitalism without 'capital'. The money of the pension funds – and of their siblings, the mutual funds – does not fit any known definition of capital; and this is not just a matter of semantics. Actually, the funds of the pension funds are deferred wages. They are being accumulated to provide the equivalent of wage income to people who no longer work.

According to Marx – that is, according to the definition of capital which was accepted by large majorities of people throughout the nineteenth and early twentieth centuries – all capital is accumulated through expropriation of the wage earner. 'Property is theft' proclaimed an early Socialist classic. Obviously this definition does not fit the capital of the pension funds in which the wage earners remain the owners of the money.

But the capital of the pension funds also does not fit any non-Marxist definition of capital. In pension-fund capitalism the wage earners finance their own employment through deferring part of their wages. Wage earners are the main beneficiaries of the earnings of capital and of capital gains. We have no social, political or economic theory that fits what has already become reality.

The governance of corporations

The most important question raised by the emergence of the pension funds (and of the other institutional investors) as the main supplier of capital and the majority owners of the large businesses is their role and function in the economy. Their emergence makes obsolete all traditional ways of managing and controlling the large business organization. This forces us to think through and redefine the *governance of corporations.*

One of the most influential American books of this century was published in 1933.* It pointed out that in the large corporation the legal owners, the shareholders, were no longer able or willing to control. Professional management controlled without ownership stake. There was no other way, Berle and Means pointed out, to finance the large corporation. It had outgrown financing by any single owner or group of owners. It required financing through the investments of large numbers of people, not one of whom could possibly own enough to control the company or even enough to be much concerned about its management. 'Property', Berle and Means pointed out, had become 'investment'. To whom, therefore, is management accountable, Berle and Means asked? And for what?

Twenty years later an attempt was made in the United States to answer these questions. The attempted answer – developed around 1950 (and first critically discussed in my 1954 book *The Practice of Management*) – was that management was a 'trustee' accountable to no one single group or person. 'Management' in the large publicly owned company, the 1950s asserted, should act 'in the best balanced interests of a number of constituencies: shareholders, employees, suppliers, plant communities, and so on' – what are now called 'stakeholders'. Management would discharge its duties by being a benevolent despot. As in all benevolent despotisms, no one tried to define what those 'best balanced interests' were or should be, let alone how performance of this 'trusteeship' could be defined or measured. Worse still, there was no attempt to make management accountable to anyone. On the contrary, boards of directors, legally the governing organ of a corporation, became increasingly impotent and increasingly rubber stamps for a company's top management.

Any government, whether that of a company or of a nation, degenerates into mediocrity and malperformance if it is not clearly accountable for results and not clearly accountable to someone. This is what happened to the big American corporations in the 30 years between 1950 and 1980.

This development then made possible the frantic financial manipulations of the 1970s and 1980s, the hostile takeovers, the

* *The Modern Corporation and Private Property,* by Adolph A. Berle and Gardner Means.

leveraged buy-outs, the acquisitions and divestments. It made possible the decade of greed and the 'bubble economy', which predictably collapsed in a series of financial scandals. But hostile takeovers and leveraged buy-outs were possible only because in the meantime institutional investors had emerged as the holders of controlling majorities in the large corporations. It was the institutional investors who financed the raiders. As trustees, the institutional investors were legally obligated to support the raiders if they offered – or seemed to offer – a little more money for shares held by the pension fund than the current stock market price.

What emerged from this frantic decade was a redefinition of the purpose and rationale of big business and of the function of management. Instead of being managed 'in the best balanced interests of stakeholders', corporations were now to be managed exclusively to 'maximize shareholders' value'. This will not work either. It forces the corporation to be managed for the shortest term. But this means damaging, if not destroying, the wealth-producing capacity of the business. It means decline, and fairly soon. Long-term results cannot be achieved by piling short-term results on short-term results. They are being obtained by balancing short-term and long-term needs and objectives. Furthermore, managing a business exclusively for the shareholders alienates the very people on whose motivation and dedication the modern business depends: the knowledge workers. An engineer will not be motivated to work to make a speculator rich.

The 'professional managers' of the 1930s were right in asserting that a business has to be managed by balancing short- and long-term results, and by balancing the interests of different constituencies, each with a genuine stake in the business. But we also now know, as we did not know 40 years ago, how to do this. In fact, we know in what areas to set objectives, and how to integrate the pursuit of goals in different areas into a focused strategy. We know how to integrate business results and financial results. We know that in a modern economy, that is, in an economy of change and innovation, there is no such thing as 'profit'. There are only costs, costs of the past – which the accountant records – and costs of an uncertain future. And the minimum financial return from the operations of the past, that is, adequate to the costs of the future, is the cost of capital. By this measurement, incidentally, all but a handful of American companies have failed to cover their costs in the last 30 years.

Making management accountable

What management should be accountable for, in other words, we now know. To whom should it be accountable? The standard answer is, of course, to the 'owners', and this would then mean the institutional investors and especially the pension funds.

But, as already said, the pension funds cannot possibly act as 'owners'. They cannot possibly manage a business. But they also can no longer consider themselves as 'investors'. An investor can always sell his or her holdings. But the holdings of large pension funds – even of medium-sized ones – are so big that they simply cannot be sold. The only market for them is other pension funds. Pension funds, in other words, can neither manage a business nor walk away from it. *They have to make sure that the business is being managed.*

We therefore can predict with high probability that within the next 20 years we are going to develop what I have been calling a 'business audit'. It will track the performance of a company and of its management against a strategic plan and against specific objectives. This will then show, over a period of a few years, whether a business performs or not. The first steps in the direction of developing such a business audit and of the institutions to administer it are already being taken. The models are the public accountants who in all developed countries routinely inspect and audit the financial performance of a business. Such a business audit will give management the autonomy which it needs to perform. And yet it will establish accountability for performance and enforce it. For it will put management under the discipline of known and public performance requirements. The business audit would at the same time enable the trustees of capital, that is, the institutional investors, to act as responsible owners whose duty it is to take care of the property in their keeping, that is, of the companies whose legal owners they represent, and as the stewards for the real owners, the future beneficiaries of the pension fund. The interests of these beneficiaries are, of course, in long-term rather than in short-term results and in the growth of the economy rather than in short-term stock market prices.

This role and function is totally different – in theory as well as in practice – from that which capital had in 'capitalism'. The function of capital will increasingly be to make knowledge effective in performance. It will increasingly serve performing management rather than dominate it.

And what should this new social structure be called? When I first discussed it, in the mid-1970s, I called it 'Pension-fund Socialism'. Might 'Employee Capitalism' be a better term?

4

The productivity of the new workforces

The new challenge facing the post-capitalist society is the productivity of knowledge workers and service workers. To improve the productivity of knowledge workers will in fact require drastic changes in the structure of the organizations of post-capitalist society and in the structure of society itself.

Forty years ago people doing knowledge work and service work were still less than one-third of the workforce. Now such people account for three-quarters (if not four-fifths) of the workforce in all developed countries – and their share is still going up. Their productivity rather than the productivity of the people who make and move things is *the* productivity of a developed economy. It is abysmally low. The productivity of people doing knowledge work and service work may actually be going down rather than going up. One-third of the capital investment in developed countries in the last 30 years has gone into equipment to handle data and information, computers, fax machines, electronic mail, closed-circuit television, and so on. Yet the number of people doing clerical work, that is, the number of people to whose work most of this equipment is dedicated, has been going up much faster than total output or GNP. Instead of becoming more productive, clerical workers have become less productive. The same is true of salespeople and also of engineers. And no one, I dare say, would maintain that the teacher of 1990 is more productive than the teacher of 1900 or the teacher of 1930.

The lowest productivity is in government employment. And yet governments everywhere are the largest employers of service workers. In the United States, for instance, one-fifth of the entire workforce is employed by federal, state and local governments, predominantly in routine clerical work. In Britain the proportion is 30%. In all developed countries government employees account for a similar share of the total workforce.

Unless we learn how to increase the productivity of knowledge workers and service workers, and increase it fast, the developed countries therefore face economic stagnation and severe social tension. People can only get paid in accordance with their productivity. Their productivity creates the pool of wealth from which wages and salaries are then paid. If productivity does not go up, let alone if it declines, higher *real* incomes cannot be paid.

Knowledge workers are likely to be able to command good incomes, regardless of their productivity or of the productivity of the total economy. They are a minority. They also have mobility. But even they, in the long run, must suffer a decline in real income unless their productivity goes up. Large numbers of service workers perform work that demands fairly low skills and relatively little education. If an economy in which service worker productivity is low tries to pay them wages considerably above what their productivity produces, inflation must erode everybody's real income. In the not so long run inflation will then also create serious social tensions. If service workers, however, are paid only according to their productivity the gap between their income and that of the 'privileged', that is, the knowledge workers, must steadily widen – again creating severe social tension.

A good deal of service work does not differ too much from the work of making and doing things. This includes such clerical jobs as data processing, billing, answering customers' inquiries, handling insurance claims, issuing drivers' licences to motorists – in fact about two-thirds of all the work done in government offices and about one-third or more of all the clerical and services work done in businesses, in universities, in hospitals and so on. This is, in effect, 'production work' which differs from that done in the factory only in that it is being done in an office. But even this work has first to be 're-engineered' before it can be made productive. It has to be studied and restructured for optimum contribution and achievement. In all other work done by the new workforces, both knowledge workers and service workers, raising productivity requires new concepts and new approaches.

In the work on productivity in making and moving things the task is given and determined. When Frederick Taylor started to study the shovelling of sand he could take it for granted that sand had to be shovelled. In a good deal of the work making and moving things the task is actually 'machine paced'. The individual worker serves the machine.

In knowledge work and in practically all service work the machine serves the worker. The task is not given. The task has to be determined. The question 'What are the expected results from this work?' is almost never raised in traditional work study and Scientific Management. But it is the key question in making knowledge workers and service workers productive. The question asks for a risk-taking decision. There are usually choices. Unless results can be clearly specified, productivity will not be achieved.

Team work and team work

There is a second major difference between the productivity of making and moving things and the productivity of knowledge work and service work. In knowledge and service work we have to decide how the work should be organized. What kind of human team is appropriate for this kind of work and its flow?

Most human work is carried out in teams: hermits are exceedingly rare. Even the most solitary artists, writers or painters depend on others for their work to become effective – the writer on an editor, a printer, a bookshop; the painter on a gallery to sell his or her work, and so on. And most of us work in far closer relationship to our team mates.

There is a great deal of talk today about 'creating team work'. This is largely misunderstanding; it assumes that the existing organization is not a team organization. And that is demonstrably false. Second, it assumes that there is only one kind of team. But, in effect, there are three kinds of teams for all human work. And for work to be productive it has to be organized in the team that is appropriate to the work itself, and its flow.*

The first kind of team is exemplified by the baseball or cricket team. It is also the kind of team that operates on a patient in the hospital. In this team all players play *on* the team but they do not play *as* a team.

Each player in a baseball or a cricket team has a fixed position which he never leaves. In baseball, the outfielders never assist each other. They will stay in their respective positions. 'If you are up at bat you are totally alone' is an old baseball saying. Similarly, the anaesthetist will not come to the assistance of the nurse or of the surgeon, and vice versa.

This team does not enjoy a good press today. In fact, when people talk about 'building teams' they usually mean that they want to move away from this kind of team. Yet the baseball – or cricket – team has great strengths which should not be discounted. Because all players occupy fixed positions, they can be given specific tasks of their own, can be measured by performance scores for each task, can be trained for each task. It is by no means accidental that both in baseball and in cricket there are statistics on every player going back for decades. The surgical team in the hospital functions the same way.

For repetitive tasks and for work for which the rules are well known, the baseball team is the ideal. And it was this model on which modern mass production, that is, the work of making and moving things, was organized, and to which it owes a great deal of its performance capacity.

The second type of team is the soccer team. It is also the team concept on which the symphony orchestra is organized and the model for the hospital team that rallies around the patient who at two in the morning goes into cardiac arrest.

On this team, too, all players have fixed positions. The tuba players in the orchestra will not take over the parts of the double basses. They stick to their tuba parts. In the crisis team at the hospital the respiratory technician will not make an incision in the chest of the patient to massage the heart. But on these teams the members work *as* a team. Each coordinates his or her part with the rest of the team.

* On various teams – and especially on the analogy between teams in business and teams in sports, see *Game Plans* by Robert Keidel (E. P. Dutton, New York, 1985).

This team requires a conductor or a coach. And the word of the conductor or coach is law. It also requires a 'score'. And it requires endless rehearsals to work well. But, unlike the baseball team, it has great flexibility if the score is clear and if the team is well led. And it can move very fast.

Finally, there is the doubles tennis team – the team also of the jazz combo or the team of the four or five senior executives who together constitute the 'President's Office'* in the large American company, or the *Vorstand* (board of management) in the German company.

This team has to be small – seven to nine people may be the maximum. In this team the players have a 'preferred' rather than a 'fixed' position. They 'cover' for one another. And they adjust themselves to the strengths and weaknesses of each other. The player in the back field in doubles tennis adjusts to the strengths and weaknesses of the partner who plays the net. And the team only functions when this adjustment to the strengths and weaknesses of the partners has become conditioned reflex, that is, when the player in the back field of the doubles tennis team starts running to 'cover' for the weak backhand of the partner at the net, the moment the ball leaves the racket of the player on the other side.

A well-calibrated team of this kind is the strongest team of all. Its total performance is greater than the sum of the individual performances of its members; for this team uses the strength of each member but minimizes the weaknesses of each. But this team requires enormous self-discipline. The members have to work together for a long time before they actually work as a 'team'.

These types of teams cannot be mixed. One cannot play baseball and soccer (or cricket and tennis) with the same team on the same field at the same time. The symphony orchestra cannot play the way a jazz combo plays. The three teams must also be 'pure'. They cannot be hybrids. And to change from one team to another is exceedingly difficult and painful. The change cuts across old, long-established and cherished human relationships. Yet any major change in the nature of the work; its tools; its flow; and its end product, may require changing the team.

---

* On this, see also the discussion of the top management job in my 1973 book *Management, Tasks, Responsibilities, Practices*.

This is particularly true with respect to any change in the flow of information.

In the baseball-type team players get their information from the situation. Each gets information appropriate to his or her task and gets it independent of the information the team-mates receive. In the symphony orchestra or the soccer team the information comes largely from the conductor or coach. They control the 'score' the team plays. In the doubles tennis team the players get their information largely from each other. This explains why the change in information technology and the move to what I have called the 'information-based organization'* made necessary massive 're-engineering'.

The new information technology underlies the strenuous efforts of American corporations in the last ten years to 're-engineer' themselves. Traditionally, most work in large American companies was organized on the baseball team model. Top management consisted of a Chief Executive Officer to whom senior functional executives 'reported', each doing a specific kind of work, running the factories, running sales, finance and so on. The Office of the President is an attempt to convert top management into a doubles tennis team – made necessary or, at least made possible, by the advent of information.

Traditionally, work on new products was done by a baseball-type team in which each function – design, engineering, manufacturing, marketing – did its own work and then passed it on to the next function. In some major American industries, e.g. pharmaceuticals or chemicals, this was changed long ago into the soccer or symphony orchestra type of team. But the American car industry retained a baseball-type team for the design and introduction of new models. Around 1970 the Japanese began to use information to switch to a soccer-type team for this work. As a result, Detroit fell way behind both in respect to the speed with which it introduced new models and to its flexibility. Since 1980 Detroit has been trying desperately to catch up with the Japanese by changing the design and introduction of new cars to a soccer-type team. And on the factory floor the availability of information – which makes possible, and in fact mandatory, the shift to 'Total Quality Management' – is forcing Detroit to change from the base-

* On this, see Chapter 14 in my 1989 book *The New Realities* (Oxford: Butterworth-Heinemann).

ball team on which the traditional assembly line has been organized to doubles tennis teams, which is the team concept underlying 'flexible manufacturing'.

Only when the appropriate type of team has been chosen and established will work on the productivity of knowledge workers and service workers become truly effective. The right team by itself does not guarantee productivity. But the wrong team destroys productivity.

The need to concentrate

Concentration on job and task is the last prerequisite for productivity in knowledge and service work. In the work on making and doing things the task is clearly defined. Workers shovelling sand, whose task Taylor studied a century ago, were not expected to bring the sand to where they could begin shovelling it. That was somebody's else's job. The farmer ploughing the field does not climb off the tractor to attend a meeting. In machine-paced work the machine concentrates the worker; the worker is servant to the machine. In knowledge work and in most service work where the machine (if any) is a servant to the worker, productivity of knowledge and service workers requires the elimination of whatever activities do not contribute to performance. They sidetrack and divert from performance. Eliminating such work may be the single biggest step towards greater productivity in knowledge and service work.

The task of nurses in hospitals is patient care. But every study shows that they spend up to three-quarters of their time on work that does not contribute to patient care. Instead, two-thirds or three-quarters of the nurse's time is typically spent filling forms. Whenever we analyse the performance of salespeople in the department store we find that they spend more than half their time on work that does not contribute towards their performance, that is, towards satisfying the customer. They spend at least half their time filling forms that serve the computer rather than the customer. Whenever we analyse the time spent by engineers we find that half their time is spent attending meetings or polishing reports which have very little (if anything) to do with their own task. This not only destroys productivity. It destroys motivation and pride.

Wherever a hospital concentrates paperwork and assigns it to a clerk who does nothing else, nurses' productivity doubles. So does their contentment. They then suddenly have time for the work they are trained and hired for, that is, for patient care. Similarly, both the productivity and satisfaction of salespeople in the department stores shoot up overnight when the paperwork is taken out of their job and concentrated with a clerk. And the same happens when engineers are relieved of 'chores' – of draughtsmen's work, of rewriting reports and memos, of attending meetings.

Knowledge workers and service workers should always be asked: Is this work necessary to *your* main task? Does it contribute to *your* performances? Does it help you do *your* job? And if the answer is 'no', the procedure or operation is a 'chore' rather than 'work'. It should either be dropped altogether or engineered into a job of its own.

Defining performance; determining the appropriate work flow; setting up the right team; and concentration on work and achievement are the *prerequisites* for productivity in knowledge work and service work. Only when they have been done can we begin the work of making productive the *individual* job and the *individual* task.

Frederick Taylor is usually criticized for not asking the workers how to do the job. He told them. But so did Elton Mayo (1880–1949), the Australian-born Harvard psychologist who in the 1920s and 1930s attempted to replace Taylor's 'Scientific Management' with 'Human Relations'. Lenin and Stalin did not consult the 'masses' either; they told them. Freud never asked patients what they thought their problem might be. And only towards the end of World War II did it occur to any High Command to consult the users – that is, the soldiers in the field – before introducing a new weapon. The nineteenth century believed in the expert knowing the answers.

By now we have learned that those who do a job know more about it than anybody else. They may not know how to interpret their knowledge. But they know what works and what doesn't. And so, in the last 40 years, we have learned that work on improving job or task begins with the people who do the work. They must be asked: What can we learn from you? What do you have to tell us about the job and how it should be done? What tools do you need? What information do you need? Workers must be required to take responsibility for their own productivity, and to exercise control over it.

We were first taught this lesson by American production in World War II.* But as is well known, the Japanese were the first to apply the idea (if only because a few Americans, especially Edwards Deming and Joseph Juran, taught it to them).

After World War II, the United States, Great Britain and Continental Europe went back, however, to the traditional 'productivity-by-command' approach – largely because of strong union opposition to anything that would give the worker a 'managerial attitude' let alone 'managerial responsibility'. In the last ten years, however, American management has rediscovered the lesson of its own performance in World War II.

In making and moving things, partnership with a responsible worker is the *best* way. But Taylor's telling them worked too, and quite well after all. In knowledge and service work, however, partnership with the responsible worker is the *only* way to improve productivity. Nothing else works at all.

Productivity in knowledge work and service work demand that we build continuous learning into the job and into the organization. As has already been said (in Chapter 2), knowledge demands continuous learning because knowledge constantly changes itself. But service work also, even of the purely clerical kind, demands continuous self-improvement – that is, continuous learning. The best way for people to learn how to be more productive is to teach. To obtain the productivity improvement which the post-capitalist society needs, the organization has to become a learning and a teaching organization.

Restructuring organizations

To improve the productivity of making and moving things required drastic changes in the organization of the work. It did

* My two books *The Future of Industrial Man* (1942) and *The New Society* (1949) were the first to draw this conclusion from the World War II experience. In these books I argued for the 'responsible worker' taking 'management responsibility'. As a result of their wartime experiences, Edwards Deming and Joseph Juran each developed what we now call 'Quality Circles' and 'Total Quality Management'. Finally, the idea was forcefully presented by Douglas McGregor in his well-known 1960 book *The Human Side of Enterprise* with his 'Theory X and 'Theory Y'.

not, however, need more than minor changes in the structure of the organization. Improving the productivity of knowledge workers and service workers will, however, demand fundamental changes in the structure of organizations. It will even require *totally new organizations.*

Re-engineering the team so that work can flow properly will lead to the elimination of most 'management layers'. In the symphony orchestra several hundred highly skilled musicians play together. But there is only one 'executive', the conductor, with no intermediate layers between him or her and the orchestra members. This will be the organization model for the information-based organization. We will thus see a radical shift from the tradition in which performance was primarily rewarded by advancement into command positions, that is, into managerial ranks. Organizations will have no (or very few) such command positions. We will increasingly see organizations operate like the jazz combo, in which leadership within the team shifts with the specific assignment and is independent of the 'rank' of each member. The word 'rank' should altogether disappear from the vocabulary of knowledge work and knowledge worker. It should be replaced by 'assignment'.

This shift will raise tremendous problems of motivation, of reward, of recognition.

The case for outsourcing

But even more drastic, indeed revolutionary, are the requirements for obtaining productivity for service workers. Service work in many cases will be contracted out of the organization to whom the service is being rendered. This particularly applies to support work, such as maintenance, and to a good deal of clerical work. Such 'outsourcing' will, moreover, be applied increasingly to such work as drafting for architects and to the technical or professional library. In fact, American law firms already contract out to an outside computerized database most of what their own law library used to do.

One driving force behind outsourcing is the need to make service workers productive. The greatest need for increased productivity is in activities which do not lead to promotions into senior management within the organization. But nobody in senior management is likely to be greatly interested in this kind of work, knows enough about it, cares greatly for it and considers it important – no matter how much money is at stake. Such work does not fit the organization's value system.

In the hospital, for instance, the value system is that of doctors and nurses. They are concerned with patient care. No one therefore pays much attention to maintenance work, support work, clerical work – even though that is where half the hospital's costs are likely to be. Nobody from these support activities will ever get into a senior hospital position.

Most of the women who start cleaning hospital floors or making hospital beds will, 15 years later, still clean hospital floors or make hospital beds. By contrast, the woman who as a senior vice president heads the hospital division of America's largest maintenance company started as an almost illiterate Mexican immigrant, with a bucket and a broom 14 years ago. But she started working in a hospital where maintenance work had been contracted out to a maintenance company. As a result, she had opportunities for advancement. But, also as a result, productivity in the hospitals maintained by this company has almost tripled in the last 15 years. The time needed to make a bed, for instance, has been cut by two-thirds.

The maintenance company has a financial interest in improving the productivity of menial jobs. It has people in executive positions who know first-hand the work needed to maintain a hospital. The company was therefore willing to work for years on the redesign of all the tools needed, including a redesign of the bed sheet. It was willing to invest substantial capital in the new methods. None of this a hospital would have done. To make hospital maintenance productive required an outside contractor.

The greatest need to outsource – whether manual work like maintenance or clerical work like billing – is in government (see Chapter 8). There productivity is lowest. There also are the most people employed in such support activities.

But large businesses are not much different. They also require systematic contracting out of service work to organizations whose business it is to do such work. These contracting organizations have career opportunities for people doing such work. Their executives take such work seriously. They are therefore willing to invest time and money in redesigning the work and its tools. They are willing, even eager, to do the hard work needed to improve productivity. Above all, they take the people who do such work seriously enough to challenge them to take leadership in improving their work and its productivity.

Outsourcing is needed not just because of the economics involved. It is required equally because it gives opportunities, income and dignity to service work and service workers.

We should, therefore, expect within a fairly short period of years to have such work contracted out to independent organizations which compete for such work and which get paid for their own effectiveness in making the work more productive.

This means a radical change in the structure of the organization of tomorrow. It means that the big business, the government agency, the large hospital, the large university will not necessarily be the one that *employs* a great many people. It will be the one that has substantial revenues and substantial results – achieved in large part because it itself does only wor˙ that is focused on its mission; work that is directly related to its results; work which it values, recognizes and appropriately rewards. The rest it contracts out.

Averting a new class conflict

The rapid increase in the productivity of the workers making and moving things overcame the ninteenth-century's nightmare of 'class conflict'. Now a rapid increase in the productivity of service workers is required to avert the danger of a new 'class conflict' – between the two new dominant groups in the post-capitalist society: knowledge workers and service workers. To make service work productive is thus the first *social* priority of the post-capitalist society – in addition to being an economic priority.

Knowledge workers and service workers are not 'classes' in the traditional sense. The line between the two is porous. In the same family there are likely to be service workers and knowledge workers who have advanced education. But there is danger that the post-capitalist society will become a class society unless service workers attain both income and dignity. This requires productivity. But it also requires opportunities for advancement and recognition.

The post-capitalist society, in its structure, will therefore be different from either capitalist or socialist society. In both, organizations tried to encompass the maximum of activities. Organizations of the post-capitalist society, by contrast, will concentrate on their core tasks. For other work they will work with other organizations in a bewildering variety of alliances and partnerships. Capitalist and socialist society were, to use a metaphor, 'crystalline' in their structure. Post-capitalist society is likely to resemble a fluid.

5

The responsibility-based organization

Political and social theory, since Plato and Aristotle, has focused on *power*. But *responsibility* must be the principle which informs and organizes the post-capitalist society. The society of organizations, the knowledge society, demands a *responsibility-based organization*.

Organizations must take responsibility for the limit of their power, that is, for the point at which exercising their functions ceases to be legitimate. Organizations must take 'social responsibility'. There is no one else around in the society of organizations to take care of society itself. Yet they must do so responsibly, that is, within the limits of their competence and without endangering their performance capacity.

Organizations, in order to function, have to have considerable power. What is legitimate power? What are the limits? What should they be?

Finally, organizations themselves must be built on responsibility within, rather than on power or on command and control.

Where right becomes wrong

In the 1930s John L. Lewis (1880–1969) was considered the sec-ond-most powerful man in America, after President Franklin D. Roosevelt. In fact, Roosevelt owed his election in large part to Lewis who, until then a life-long Republican, led his coal miners union (the UMW) and with it the entire American labour move-ment into the Democratic camp at the 1932 Convention. He then led the unionization drive of the New Deal years and became the head of the new and powerful labour organization, the Congress of Industrial Organizations.

But in 1943 Lewis rebelled against the wage freeze imposed during World War II and pulled his coal miners out on strike. President Roosevelt appealed to him to heed the national interest and to call off the strike. But Lewis refused. 'The President of the United States,' he said 'is paid to look after the national interest. I am paid to look after the interests of the miners.'

War production was then just starting up. American soldiers were already in combat, both in Europe and in the Pacific. But woefully they still lacked equipment and ammunition; they were suffering heavy casualties because of these shortages. The entire war effort was fuelled by coal and the country could not afford to lose even one day's coal production. Furthermore, the miners were the highest-paid workers in America; compared to the pay of the men in uniform they were plutocrats.

But Lewis won the strike.

He immediately lost, however, all power, all influence, all respect – even within the labour movement, and indeed even within his own union. The UMW itself immediately began to decline – in power, in influence, in membership. Ten years later coal strikes had become non-events. In fact, Lewis's 1943 victory marked the begin-ning of the decline of unionism in the United States.

Lewis lived long enough to see the consequences of his victory. But he maintained to his dying day that he was right in calling the strike, that it was his duty to do so. 'What is good for labour,' he repeatedly said, 'is ultimately good for the country. And a war is the only time when labour is needed, the only time when it has any real power, the only time when its legitimate claims for decent pay can be successfully pressed.' He could never, it is reported, understand why the American public did not agree.

This is, of course, an extreme case. But it is also a revealing case. Lewis *knew* that he was in the right. But at what point does the right of an organization turn into social wrong; at what point is its function no longer legitimate?

These days there is a great deal of concern in the United States about 'business ethics'. But most of the discussion – and the courses under this title taught in business schools – deal with *wrong*doing, e.g. with giving bribes or with covering up for defective or harmful products. That wrongdoers in high places always plead their allegiance to a 'higher good' is nothing new. And all that needs to be said on the subject was said 350 years ago by the great French mathematician/philosopher Blaise Pascal (1626–1662) in his 1655 book *Letters to a Provincial*, which demolished once and for all the Jesuit ethics of casuistry, that is, the plea for a special ethics of power.

But the Lewis story does not deal with 'wrong against wrong'. It deals with 'right against right'. While not totally unprecedented, this is a new problem. It may be considered the central problem of responsibility within the Society of Organizations.

To be able to perform, an organization and its people must believe – as John L. Lewis did – that its own specialized task is the most important task in society. As said earlier, hospitals must believe that nothing matters as much as curing the sick. Businesses must believe that nothing matters as much as satisfying the material wants and needs of the community; and, in particular, that no product or service is nearly as vital to economy and community as the product or service 'our' business produces and delivers. Unions must believe that nothing matters except the rights of the working man. Churches must believe that nothing matters except faith. Schools must believe that education is the one absolute good, and so on.

These organizations must be self-centred. Collectively they discharge the tasks of society. But each discharges only one task, sees only one task.

In fact, we expect the leaders of these organizations to believe, as Lewis did, that their organization is *the* organization, that it *is* society.

During his lifetime, Charles E. Wilson (1890–1961) was a prominent personality on the American scene, first as President and Chief Executive Officer of General Motors, the world's largest and most successful manufacturer at that time, and then, from 1953 to 1957, as Secretary of Defense in the Eisenhower Administration. If he is remembered at all today it is, however, for something he did *not* say: 'What is good for General Motors is good for the United States.' What Wilson did say in his 1953 confirmation hearings for the Defense Department job was: 'What is good for the United States is good for GM.' Wilson tried all the remaining years of his life to correct the misquote. But no one listened to him. Everyone argued: 'If he didn't say it, he surely believes it – in fact, he should believe it.'

Where, then, are the limits? In an emergency such as a war or a great natural catastrophe the answer is fairly simple: the survival of society comes before the survival of any one of its organs. But outside of such crises there are no hard-and-fast answers. The only way therefore to approach the problem is as the joint responsibility of the leaders of our organizations.

The closest approach so far is probably that of Japanese big business in the post-World War II period. In their planning during those years the business leaders started out with the question: 'What is best for Japan, its society, its economy?' They then asked: 'And how can we turn this into an opportunity for business in general and for *our* business in particular?' They were not 'altruistic' or 'selfless'; on the contrary, they were extremely profit-conscious. They did not 'take leadership'. They accepted responsibility. But even in Japan business and its leaders became self-centred again once their country fully emerged from post-war reconstruction and into economic world leadership.

What is social responsibility?

The organizations of the Society of Organizations are special-purpose organs. Each is good at only one task; and this specialization alone gives them their capacity to perform.

Organizations can only do damage to themselves and to society if they tackle tasks that are beyond their specialized competence, their specialized values, their specialized function. The American hospital did a good deal of harm to itself and little good to the community when it took on the inner city's social ills in the 'inner city clinic'. The American school has failed miserably to produce racial integration. The causes are undoubtedly good. They cry out for action, e.g. for desegregation in America. But the needed action – or at least the action chosen by these various organizations – was beyond the organizations' focus and function, and totally beyond their competence.

And yet who else is there to take care of society, its problems and its ills? These organizations collectively *are* society. It is futile to argue, as does the American economist and Nobel Laureate Milton Friedman (born 1912), that a business has only one responsibility: economic performance. Economic performance is the *first* responsibility of a business. A business that does not show a profit at least equal to its cost of capital is socially irresponsible. It wastes society's resources. Economic performance is the basis; without it a business cannot discharge any other responsibilities, cannot be a good employer, a good citizen, a good neighbour.

But economic performance is not the *only* responsibility of a business. Nor is educational performance the only responsibility of a school or health-care performance the only responsibility of a hospital. Power must always be balanced by responsibility; otherwise it is tyranny. But without responsibility power also always degenerates into non-performance. And organizations do have power, albeit only social power.

The demand for the social responsibility of organizations will not go away. Hitherto we have talked mainly of the social responsibility of *business* – for a simple reason: business was the first of the new organizations to emerge. We will increasingly concern ourselves with the social responsibilities of other organizations: above all, with that of the university, which has a social monopoly – a power no other institution ever had before, as will be discussed shortly.

We do know, if only in rough outline, what the answer to the social responsibility problem has to be. An organization has full responsibility for its impacts on community and society, e.g. for the effluents it discharges into a local river or for the traffic jam its work schedules create on the city streets. It is, however, irresponsible of an organization to accept, let alone to pursue, responsibilities that would seriously impede its capacity to perform its main task and mission. And where it has no competence it has no responsibility.

But – and it is a big 'but' – organizations of the Society of Organizations have a responsibility to try to find an approach to basic social problems which fits their competence and which, indeed, makes the social problem into an opportunity for the organization.

Power and organizations

There is another limit to the social action of the organizations: they are *social* institutions. They have neither legitimacy nor competence in *politics*.

The organizations of post-capitalist society all want things from the political power, the government. But they want things that are of benefit to them, enable them – at least in their opinion – better to do their own job, fit into their value system or line their pockets. But they are not and should not be concerned with political power for themselves. They are concerned with function.

This is in striking contrast to all earlier pluralist societies. They all were pluralisms of *competing* power centres. The pluralism of the Society of Organization is one of discrete organizations, operating in parallel rather than in competition. The business enterprise does not compete with the hospital for patients or for the patronage of physicians; and the hospital in turn does not try to sell computers in competition with IBM. Each is the other's supplier and customer. The barons, counts, dukes, and bishops of medieval Europe – or the *Daimyos* of medieval Japan – constantly waged war on each other. Modern organizations *lobby*.

In fact, nothing is as damaging for an organization as an attempt at political power. It always ends in disaster. In Argentina, Brazil and Peru the army was the most highly respected institution in each country until it seized power during the 1960s and 1970s. In each case the military took action only because the country was on the point of total collapse. In each case they came into power with substantial, perhaps even overwhelming, popular support. But in each case when they relinquished power, they had become corrupted, discredited, demoralized and almost destroyed.

In twentieth-century demonology a popular figure has been the sinister business executive plotting for political power. But no successful business executive – neither J. P. Morgan, nor Rockefeller, nor Krupp nor any of the other 'tycoons' – was ever interested in power; they were interested in products, markets, revenues.

Businessmen who try to enter politics after a successful business career are not uncommon – though rarely successful. But I know of only two businessmen – both German: Hugo Stinnes (1870–1924) and Alfred Hugenberg (1965–1951) – who tried to use their business position to dominate government and politics; Stinnes in the early 1920s, Hugenberg a few years later. Both did immeasurable damage to the Weimar Republic, and are largely responsible for Hitler's eventual triumph. But both failed politically; and the attempt at political power in the end destroyed both their businesses and the men themselves.

Even union leaders destroy themselves and their union when they reach for political power.

In the early 1970s the leader of the British coal miners union (the NUM), Arthur Scargill (born 1938), seemed England's most powerful man. In 1974 he called a strike to break the Tory government and to establish himself as the country's most powerful politician. Just as John L. Lewis had done 30 years earlier in the US, he won the strike; the government actually fell. But Scargill was finished, and so was his union. Ten years later, he again called a strike to re-establish his power and to defeat another Conservative prime minister. Margaret Thatcher (born 1925) broke the strike with overwhelming public support, which even included a good many of Scargill's own miners. All Scargill accomplished was to enable Mrs Thatcher to enact legislation sharply curtailing the power of unions and union leaders.

Yet the union is the most nearly political of all the major organizations of the Society of Organizations. It has to be. It cannot exist, let alone prosper, unless government supports it. Very few, if any, union gains in developed countries have been attained by union action alone; most have been attained through legislation. But even unions succeed only if they use their strength to further the 'cause of the working man', that is, if they use it to carry out their *function*.

Still, the organization has *social* power – and must have social power – and a good deal of it. It needs power to make decisions about people – whom to hire, whom to fire, whom to promote. It needs power to establish the rules and the discipline needed to produce results – e.g. assignments of jobs and tasks to individuals and the establishment of working hours. It needs power to decide which factories to build and where, and which to close. It needs power to set prices.

Non-business organizations actually have the greatest social power. Few organizations in history have been granted the power today's university has. Refusal to admit or to grant the diploma is tantamount to debarring a person from access to career and opportunities. Similarly, the power of the American hospital to deny a physician hospital privileges virtually excludes that physician from practising medicine. A union's power to deny admission to apprenticeship or its control of access to employment in a closed shop where only union members can be hired similarly gives the union tremendous social power.

This power can be regulated, limited and restrained by the political power. It can be made subject to due process and to review by the law courts. But the social power of organizations cannot be exercised by the political authorities. It must be exercised by the individual organization.

The first answer to this problem is that no organization must be allowed power unless absolutely necessary to the discharge of its function. Anything beyond this is usurpation.

A second answer is that the exercise of the organization's legitimate power must be safeguarded against abuse of power. There must be clear and public rules for its exercise, and there must be review and appeal to some one or some tribunal that is impartial and not part of the problem. There must be what lawyers call 'due process'.

The Bishop has far more power over the priests of his Catholic diocese than most chief executive officers of other organizations. But he cannot remove a priest from his parish or fire him. This can be done only by the Diocesan Court and only 'for cause'. And while the Bishop appoints the members of the court, he cannot remove them during their fixed term of office.

But the most important answer to the problem of the power of the organization is conversion from the power-based to the responsibility-based organization. It is the only answer, moreover, that fits the *knowledge organization*.

When modern organizations first arose 130 years ago they were modelled after the first, and at that time the most successful, of the new organizations – the army – as it had been restructured in Prussia between 1855 and 1865. That army was, of necessity, based on command and control. A very small number of highly trained people at the top commanded a very large number of unskilled people drilled in a few repetitive motions. The Prussian Army which won such easy victories over Austria and France – both fielding larger forces and the second one also better armed – was, in effect, an 'assembly line', and a highly efficient one. Such knowledge as it needed was provided by special 'staffs' (i.e. the renowned Prussian General Staff) which were separate from the 'line', that is, from doing.

This organization structure reached its peak in the late 1920s. Those years saw both its extension into all kinds of non-military work, and the development of more and more specialized staffs.

World War II was decided in the last analysis by the success of the United States in projecting a command and control organization into the economic sphere, that is, into industrial production and into logistics.

But by World War II it had also become clear that the command and control organization was rapidly becoming outdated and was no longer adequate to the needs of the future. It was also becoming clear that the much-publicized attempt of those years to modify the command and control model by giving the worker a 'feeling' of responsibility – the essence of the Harvard-based 'Human Relations' school – was not going to succeed. Far more was needed than psychological manipulation.

In those years I first began to talk of the 'responsible worker' who would have a 'managerial attitude' and take 'managerial responsibility' in my 1942 book *The Future of Industrial Man* and my 1949 book *The New Society* (both about to be reissued by Transaction Publishers). But only in Japan did industry pay heed, and even there only to a limited extent. It was actually in the military that the transformation of organization first began. To this day, the military, especially in the United States, has gone furthest in changing organization from being based on command and control to being based on responsibility.

From command to information

By 1970 information began to transform organizations. We soon learned that the introduction into organization of information as a structural and organic element means the elimination of many (if not of most) layers of management. In the traditional organization most people called managers do not actually manage. They relay orders downwards and information upwards. When information becomes available, they become redundant.

The right model for the information-based organization is not the military, even in its modified form. It is the symphony orchestra, in which each player plays directly and without intermediary to the 'chief executive', the conductor, and can do so because everybody has the same 'score', that is, the same information. Or it is the jazz combo in which each player takes responsibility for the 'score'.

We have to go, however, well beyond the information-based organization. We have to move to the responsibility-based organization. In knowledge work the organization is increasingly composed of specialists. Each of them knows more about his or her own specialty than anybody else in the organization. The old-type organization assumed that the superior knew what the subordinate was doing. For the superior, only a few years earlier, had occupied the subordinate's position. The knowledge-based organization has to assume, however, that superiors do not know the job of their subordinates. They have never held it.

Conductors may not know how the oboe does its work. But they know what the oboe should contribute. The surgeon similarly knows what the anaesthetist should contribute even though he or she cannot tell the anaesthetist how to do the job. Both conductor and surgeon can still appraise the performance of their team-mates. But in knowledge-based organizations there is frequently no one who knows enough of the work of the specialist to appraise what the specialist contributes. Marketing people are not knowledgeable enough to appraise the performance of market researchers. They do not even understand the researchers' language or their statistical techniques.

Sales managers are also unlikely ever to have done any sales forecasting or any pricing. They may not know enough to tell forecasters and pricers what to do. Similarly, hospital administrators may have never done clinical testing and cannot tell the pathologist in the medical laboratory what good testing is and how it should be done. In today's military the commanding officer of an air squadron may not be able to tell his crew chief what good maintenance means let alone how to do it. Even on the factory floor, especially in highly automated production, workers increasingly have more knowledge of their job than their supervisor.

From information to responsibility

The knowledge-based organization therefore requires that everyone take responsibility for objectives, contribution – and, indeed, for behaviour as well.

This implies that *all* members of the organization think through their objectives and their contribution and take responsibility for both. It implies that there are no 'subordinates'; there are only 'associates'. Furthermore, in the knowledge-based organization all members have to be able to control their own work by feed-back from their results to their objectives. (What 40 years ago, in my 1954 book *The Practice of Management*, I called 'Management by Objectives and *Self Control*'.) It also requires that all members ask themselves: 'What is the one *major contribution* to this organization and its mission which I can make at this particular time?' It requires, in other words, that all members act as responsible decision makers. All members have to see themselves as 'executives'.

It is the responsibility also of all members to communicate their objectives, their priorities and their intended contribution to their fellow workers – up, down and sideways. And it is the responsibility of all members to make sure that their own objectives fit in with the objectives of the entire group.

This responsibility for thinking through what the contribution should be, that is, for thinking through one's own responsibility as a knowledge worker, rests on each individual. In the knowledge organization it is everybody's responsibility, regardless of his or her particular job.

The 97 technicians in the steel-making minimill are legally 'workers'. But they control the machines which turn out as much steel as a conventional integrated steel mill does with a thousand people. Every one of these technicians constantly makes critical decisions at his or her computerized workstation. They can be trained – they need to be trained. But they cannot be commanded. Each makes decisions all the time that have a greater impact on the results of the entire minimill than even middle managers ever had in the conventional steel mill. Each of them has to be asked 'What should we hold *you* accountable for?' Each of them also has to be asked 'What information do *you* need'? and, in turn, 'What information do *you* owe the rest of us?' This then means that each worker has to be a participant in the decision what equipment is needed; how the work should be scheduled; and indeed what the basic business policy of the entire mill should be. In the minimill the entire group is *one* team in which each member has responsibility for the performance of the organization.

Even organizations which, at first glance, do only low-skilled (if not unskilled) work need to be restructured as responsibility-based organizations. A small number of companies – one in Denmark, one in the United States, one in Japan – have been successful in greatly increasing the productivity of people who do unskilled (indeed menial) work such as maintenance workers in hospitals, in factories, in office buildings. They have achieved these productivity increases by demanding responsibility from the lowliest of their employees, from the people who start with a bucket and a broom to clean floors, or from people who clean offices after hours – for objectives, for contribution, for the performance of the entire team. These people *know* more about the job than anybody else. And being held responsible, they act responsibly.

To make everybody a contributor

There is a great deal of talk today about 'entitlement' and 'empowerment'. These terms express the demise of the command and control-based organization. But they are as much terms of power and terms of rank as the old terms were. We should instead be talking about responsibility and contribution. For power without responsibility is not power at all; it is irresponsibility.

What we should aim at is to make people responsible. What we should ask is not 'What should you be entitled to?' but 'What should you be responsible for?' The job of management in the knowledge-based organization is not to make everybody a *boss*. The task is to make everyone a *contributor*.

Part Two

Polity

6

From nation state to Megastate

In post-capitalist society the changes in political structure and polity (to use the old – but perfect – term for political society and political system) are fully as great as the changes in society and social structure. They are worldwide. And they are fully as much accomplished fact.

Yesterday's world order is going fast while tomorrow's world order has yet to emerge. We, therefore, are not facing the 'new world order' which today's politicians constantly invoke. We are facing a *new world disorder* – no one can know for how long.

In political structure and polity, too, we are moving into a 'post' age, the age of the post-sovereign state. We already know the new forces – and they are quite different from those that governed political structure and polity for the past 400 years. We know the new demands and can delineate some of them – maybe most. We do not, however, know the answers, the solutions, the new integrations. Even more than in society and social structure, the players on the stage – politicians, diplomats, civil servants, political scientists and political writers – speak and write in yesterday's terms and, by and large, act – indeed, have to act – on yesterday's assumptions and on the basis of yesterday's realities.

The paradox of the nation state

Everybody knows, and every history book teaches, that the last 400 years of world history were the centuries of the Western nation state. And for once, what everybody knows is true – but it is paradoxical truth.

For the great political thrusts in these four centuries were all attempts to transcend the nation state and to replace it with a transnational political system, whether a colonial empire or a European (or Asian) superstate. These were the centuries in which the great colonial empires rose and fell – the Spanish and Portuguese empires emerging in the sixteenth and collapsing in the early nineteenth century; then, beginning in the seventeenth century and continuing into the twentieth, the English, Dutch, French and Russian empires. As soon as a new major player emerged on the stage of world history during these four centuries he immediately set about transcending the nation state and transforming it into an empire – Germany and Italy, barely unified, went in for colonial expansion between 1880 and World War I, with Italy trying again as late as the 1930s. Even the United States became a colonial power in the early twentieth century. And so did the one non-Western country to become a nation state – Japan.

In Europe itself, the home of the nation state, these four centuries were dominated by one attempt after the other to establish a transnational superstate. Six times in this period did one European nation state attempt to become the ruler of Europe and to transform the nation state into a European superstate under its control and domination.

The first such attempt was made by Spain, beginning in the middle of the sixteenth century – when Spain itself was only emerging as a unified nation out of a congeries of squabbling kingdoms, duchies, counties and free cities, precariously held together in the person of the Prince. And Spain did not give up the dream of being master of Europe until a hundred years later, when she had all but ruined herself economically and militarily.

Almost immediately, France, first under Richelieu then under Louis XIV, took off where Spain had ended – again, to give up 75 years later, totally exhausted, especially financially. This did not, however, deter another French ruler, Napoleon, only 75 years later, to try again and to subject all of Europe to 20 years of war and turmoil in his bid to become the rule of Europe and to build a French-dominated European superstate. Then in this century came the two German wars for mastery of Europe, and, after Hitler's defeat, Stalin's attempt to create, by force of arms and by subversion, a Russian-ruled Europe. And just as Japan had tried to build a Western-style colonial empire as soon as she had become a nation state, she also followed the Western example and tried, in this century, to create a Japanese-ruled Asian superstate.

In fact, it was not the nation state that begat the empires. The nation state itself arose as a response to transnational drives. The Spanish empire in the Americas produced so much gold and silver that Spain, under Philip II, Charles V's son and successor, could finance the first standing army since the Roman legions, the Spanish Infantry – arguably the first 'modern' organization. Thus equipped, Spain launched the first campaign for the mastery of Europe, the first attempt to unify Europe under Spanish rule. Countering Spain's threat became the motivation and avowed aim of the inventor of the nation state, the French lawyer-politician Jean Bodin (1530–1591), in his 1576 book *Six Livres de la République*. It was the Spanish threat that made Bodin's nation state the 'progressive' cause throughout Europe. And it was only because the threat was so great and so real that Bodin's recommendations were accepted: the nation state and its institutions; a centrally controlled civil service answerable only to the sovereign; central control of the military and a standing army officered by professional soldiers appointed by and accountable to central government; central control of coinage, taxes, customs; a centrally appointed professional judiciary rather than courts staffed by local magnates. Each of them threatened a powerfully entrenched 'special interest' of earlier times: an autonomous Church and exempt bishoprics and abbeys; local lords of all sizes, each with his own armed retainers owing fealty only to him, and each with his own jurisdiction and his own taxing powers; free cities and self-governing trade guilds, and scores of others. But the Spanish bid for mastery of Europe left no alternative to them; it was either subjection to the national sovereign or conquest by a foreign sovereign. From then on, practically every change in the political structure of the European nation state was caused – or at least triggered – by similar attempts to gain the mastery of Europe and to replace the nation state by a superstate dominated in turn by France, Germany or Russia.

One might therefore expect political scientists to have studied the colonial empire and to have developed a political theory for it. They have done neither. They have focused on the political theory and institutions of the nation state. One should have expected historians similarly to have studied the European superstates. But in every university the prestigious chairs of history are chairs of *national* history. The famous history books all deal with the nation state, whether England or France, the United States or Spain, Germany, Italy or Russia. Even in Britain, ruler of the biggest and, for many years, the most successful, colonial empire, the study and teaching of history centre on the nation state.

The United States is practically alone in having produced a first-rate historian concerned with empire rather than with nation state: William Prescott (1796–1859), in his histories of the Spanish conquests of Mexico and Peru. One French historian of the first rank, Fernand Braudel (1902–1985), did not confine himself to studying the nation state. His vision took in all of Europe – and, indeed, the world altogether; but he was an economic and social rather than a political historian. The greatest nineteenth-century German historians – the two who more than anyone else established history as a 'science' – Leopold von Ranke (1795–1886) and Theodor Mommsen (1817–1903), did not confine themselves to writing German history. One of Ranke's main works, for instance, was a history of the Popes. And Mommsen's great work was the history of Rome. But even they ignored the thrust towards empire in modern politics and treated the bids for the mastery of Europe as part of national history, i.e. German or French or Italian history, rather than as events transcending the nation state and indeed as attempts to replace it by a transnational political structure.

One reason for this neglect of empire and superstate: neither developed institutions. To be sure, the House of Lords in London was the ultimate court of appeal for all British possessions. But this was quite incidental to its sitting as the Court of Appeal for the British Isles. Similarly, the British Parliament was in theory the legislative body for all British possessions. But all its members were elected from the 'United Kingdom', that is, from the British Isles only. It very rarely – and then only in times of crisis – concerned itself with anything but United Kingdom affairs. King or Queen reigned over the entire British Empire; yet no British monarch set foot in any British possession until after they had ceased to be British possessions, that is, after the Empire had disappeared (when the present Queen, Elizabeth II, began to visit former Empire countries). Yet Britain came closer to building an 'empire' than any other country.

The colonial 'empires' were not fiction. But they were not empires. They were nation states with colonial possessions. One need only compare them with the political structure from which they took their name: The Empire of the Romans. The age of the colonial empires lasted almost exactly as long as the Roman Empire – 400 years. There should thus have been more than enough time for political, social, economic integration of mother country and empire. But none was even attempted.

The three greatest Roman Emperors after Augustus – Trajan (reigned AD 98–117), Hadrian (reigned AD 117–138) and Diocletian (reigned AD 284–305) – were 'colonials'; Trajan and Hadrian were born and raised in Spain, Diocletian in the former Yugoslavia. They were not of Latin stock; the first two were probably Berbers, Diocletian an Illyrian or a Slav. But can one imagine the American George Washington (1732–1799), the South African Jan Smuts (1875–1950) or the Indian Nawaharlal Nehru (1889–1969) as British prime ministers? Yet they were surely the ablest and most prominent English-speaking and English-cultured political leaders of their time, that is, respectively at the end of the eighteenth century, after World War I and after Churchill's defeat in the general election following World War II.

Of the two last great writers of classical Latin, one, St Augustine (AD 354–430), was born and raised in the interior of what is now Algeria and was probably of Berber descent. His contemporary, St Jerome (AD 340–420), was a Slovene, born not far from present Ljubljana. He spent his formative years in German Trier and did his most important work, the translation of the Bible into Latin, while living in Jerusalem and Bethlehem. The most enduring legacy of the Roman Empire – it still underpins European law and jurisprudence – was the codification of the laws (the *Codex Iuris Civilis*) written in Latin. But it was compiled in Greek-speaking Constantinople, at the behest of a Greek-speaking emperor, Justinian (AD 483–565), by scholars not one of whom was himself a Roman, and at a time when the Latin-speaking West of the Empire had already succumbed to the Barbarians.

And for hundreds of years, after Rome's fall, educated persons in the former Empire, even the most devout of Christians, thought of themselves as Romans, educated themselves in the Latin of

Cicero and yearned back to the 'glory that was Rome', to Augustus, Trajan, Hadrian.

There were a good many settlers in the American Thirteen Colonies – especially among the 'Better Kind' – who considered themselves 'Englishmen', rather than 'Americans' during the American War of Independence, that is, during the first break-up of one of the modern empires. But these American 'Loyalists' were the exception. Few 'Colonials' in Mexico, Colombia or Brazil mourned the passing of the Spanish and Portuguese Empires. And even fewer 'Colonials' mourned the disappearance of the twentieth-century empires, those of the British, the French, the Dutch, the Japanese. The British Raj in India gave birth to a remarkably large and distinguished upper class of truly bicultural people, many of them educated at the best English universities and all of them steeped in English poetry, in Shakespeare, in English law and English constitutional philosophy and history. Yet not one of these held fast to the Empire or to the Imperial connection. Not one tried to find a constitutional solution to preserve the cultural community of Empire while establishing Indian political autonomy. Instead they became the most dedicated, most uncompromising agitators for Indian independence and for a separate Indian national state.

Even more amazing is the lack of integration in the Russian Empire. Ukrainians, White Russians, Armenians, Georgians, Germans – indeed people of every European stock (except only Jews and Catholic Poles) – had for centuries been treated as equals, in both the Russia of the Tsar and the Russia of the Communists. All they had to do was to learn Russian. A large number of Tsarist generals and ministers were of German origin, e.g. Count Witte, the reform-minded prime minister of the last Tsar. Stalin was a Georgian; and the last chief of staff of the Soviet Army was a Ukrainian. Yet as the Soviet Empire dissolves there is virtually no pro-Empire sentiment, no pro-Empire party, no pro-Empire movement. Resistance has been entirely in the name of nationalism rather than in that of Empire. Ethnic Russians, living in what was becoming a new national state, e.g. Moldova or Latvia, protest against being made Moldovans or Latvians and demand independence of their own.

This inability of the colonial empires to become anything more than administrative abstractions, that is, their inability to become political societies, is all the more paradoxical as they all came into being so very easily – one is tempted to say 'naturally'. While the Roman Empire was established in bloody war after bloody war, modern colonial empires were established with a minimum of fighting. To be sure, the British fought in India – but primarily against the French rather than against Indian rulers. They fought a bitter war against the Boers in South Africa. But otherwise the British Empire was established with little violence except for local skirmishes, each involving no more than a thousand or so British fighting men. The Indian Mutiny of 1857 was the only major uprising against British rule in the 150 years between American Independence and the secession of Ireland after World War I.

Similarly the only prolonged resistance the Russians encountered against the extension of their empire was in the Caucasus – not in the Ukraine, not in the Baltic States (annexed in the eighteenth century), not in Central Asia. The battles the French had to fight to establish their Empire in South-east Asia and in Africa were similarly mere skirmishes involving fewer soldiers than France – or any European country – committed to trivial and insignificant European border conflicts.

And yet the moment a European power (or Japan) showed any sign of weakness, its empire collapsed; and it collapsed into nation states. Even the 'White Dominions' of the British Empire – Australia, Canada, New Zealand – proud though they are of their English heritage and cultural tradition – became nation states the moment they ceased to be 'colonies'. No other form of political integration was available.

Modern empire lacked integrative power. The nation state alone could integrate, could form a polity – i.e. a political society – could create citizenship.

In Europe, too, none of would-be conquerors could integrate the superstate into a political structure. All they could do – from Philip II to Stalin – was subjugate by brute force. Yet three of the attempts to create a European superstate were accompanied by ideologies with powerful appeal: Napoleon's attempt by *Liberté, Fraternité, Egalité*, the ideology of the French Revolution; Hitler's by the ideology of hate, envy and Anti-Semitism (having far more appeal than we like to admit, which, in large part, explains why there was appeasement of, rather than resistance to, Hitler in every Continental country until he had conquered it); and Stalin's by the ideology of Marxist Socialism which, for a hundred years, had the strongest and widest appeal since Christianity. Even the

Japanese attempt to create a Pan-Asian superstate was based on a powerful ideology, anti-Western and anti-colonialism. Yet all these attempts floundered on their inability to convert the conquered territories into a political structure, the failure to build political institutions, the failure to create anything even remotely comparable to St Paul's claim *Civis Romanus Sum* (I am a Roman citizen). Paul was a Jew by religion and race, a Greek by culture and language; but 'I am a Roman citizen' was a higher claim, both an appeal to a higher law and an assertion of a political identity superseding geography, race and language.

All modern empires and all superstates foundered because of their inability to transcend the nation state, let alone to become its successor.

But while the nation state thus was the one political reality in the centuries of empires and superstates, it transformed itself profoundly in the last hundred years. *It mutated into the Megastate.*

The dimensions of the Megastate

By 1870 the nation state had triumphed everywhere – even Austria had become Austria-Hungary, a federation of two nation states. And the nation states of 1870 still looked and acted like the sovereign nation state Bodin had invented 300 years earlier.

But the nation state of 1970, a century later, bore little resemblance to Bodin's state, or, indeed, to the nation state of 1870. It had mutated into the *Megastate* – the same species perhaps, as its 1870 progenitor but as different from it as panther differs from pussy cat.*

The national state was designed to be the guardian of civil society. The Megastate became its master. And in its extreme, totalitarian, form, it replaced civil society altogether. In totalitarianism all society became political society.

The national state was designed to protect both the citizen's life and liberty and the citizen's property against arbitrary acts of the sovereign. The Megastate, even in its least extreme Anglo-American form, considers a citizen's property to be held only at

---

* The first to understand this was not a political scientist or a politician, but a novelist. Franz Kafka's (1853–1924) two novels, the *Trial* and *The Castle* – both only published after his death – are the most penetrating analyses of the Megastate, as they were the earliest.

the discretion of the tax collector. As Joseph Schumpeter (1883–1950) first pointed out in his 1918 essay *Der Steuerstaat* (*The Fiscal State*), the Megastate asserts that citizens hold only what the state, expressly or tacitly, allows them to keep.

Bodin's national state had as its first function the maintenance of civil society, especially in wartime. This is, in effect, what 'defence' meant. The Megastate has increasingly blurred the distinction between peace and war. Instead of peace, there is 'Cold War'.

The Nanny State

The shift from the national state to the Megastate began in the last decades of the nineteenth century. The first small step towards the Megastate was Bismarck's invention in the 1880s of the Welfare State. Bismarck's goal was to combat the rapidly rising socialist tide. It was a response to the threat of class war. Until Bismarck, government had been seen exclusively as a political agency. Bismarck made government into a social agency. His own welfare measures – health insurance; insurance against industrial accidents; old-age pensions (followed 30 years later after World War I by the British invention of unemployment benefit) were modest enough. But the principle was radical; and it is the principle that has had far greater effect than the individual actions taken in its name.

In the German health insurance system all employed people and their families have to be insured against illness but with free choice of insurance company, most of whom are non-governmental. Unemployment benefit, as the British instituted it, made the state the insurance company; but again the state acted purely as a fiscal agency. Social Security, which brought the Welfare State to the United States in 1935-1936, was organized on the same principle. By and large, so were the other social measures of the New Deal, e.g. farm subsidies, or payments for putting land into the 'soil bank', thus ensuring both reductions in surplus production of farm crops and welfare payments to the farmers.

In the 1920s and 1930s Communists, Fascists and Nazis took over social institutions. But in the democracies government still only insured or, at most, offered payments. By and large, it still stayed out of *doing* social work or of forcing citizens into proper social behaviour.

This changed rapidly after World War II. From being a provider the state became a *manager*. The last of the traditional welfare state measures – and arguably the most successful one – was the US GI Bill of Rights, enacted right after World War II. It gave every returning American veteran the means to attend a college and to acquire higher education. The government did, however, not attempt to dictate which college to attend. It did not attempt to run any college. It offered money if the veteran choose to go to college. The veteran then decided where to go and what to study. And no college had to accept any applicant.

The other major social programme of the immediate post-war period, the British National Health Service, was the first (outside of the totalitarian countries) to take government beyond being insurer or provider. But only in part. For standard medical care, government in the National Health Service is an insurance company. It reimburses the doctor who takes care of a patient. But the doctor does not become a government employee. Nor is the patient in any way limited as to what doctor to choose.

Hospitals, however, and hospital care under the National Health Service were taken over by government. The people working in hospitals became government employees; and government actually manages the hospitals. This was the first step towards a changed role for government in the social sphere. Government ceased to be the rule setter, the facilitator, the insurer, the disbursement agent. It became the doer and the manager.

By 1960 it had become accepted doctrine in all developed Western countries that government is the appropriate doer for *all* social problems and *all* social tasks. In fact, non-governmental, private activity in the social sphere became suspect; good 'liberals' considered it 'reactionary' or 'discriminatory'. In the United States government became the actual doer in the social sphere, especially in the attempt to change human behaviour in a multiracial society by government action or government order. Only in the United States outside of totalitarian countries has government so far attempted to command changes in social values and individual behaviour.

The Megastate as master of the economy

By the late nineteenth century the nation state was being made over into an economic agency. The first steps were taken in the United States. It invented both governmental regulation of business and governmental ownership of the new businesses of a capitalist economy. Beginning in the 1870s, the United States gradually established regulation of business: banking, railways, electric power, telephones. Such government regulation – one of the most original political inventions of the nineteenth century, and a hugely successful one at first – was clearly seen from the beginning as a 'third way' between 'Unfettered Capitalism' and 'Socialism', and as a response to the tensions and problems created by the rapid spread of Capitalism and technology.

A few years later, the United States began to take businesses into government ownership – first in the 1880s in the State of Nebraska under the leadership of William Jennings Bryan (1860–1929). Another few years later, between 1897 and 1900, Karl Lueger (1844–1910), Mayor of Vienna, similarly expropriated and took into municipal ownership the street-car companies and the electric power and gas companies of the Austrian capital. Like Bismarck, who had acted to combat Socialism, neither Bryan nor Lueger were socialists. Both were what the United States calls 'Populists'. Both saw in government ownership primarily a means of assuaging a rapidly escalating class war between 'Capital' and 'Labour'.

Still few people in the nineteenth century – indeed few people before 1929 – believed that government should or could manage the economy, let alone that government should or could control recessions and depressions. Most economists believed that a market economy is 'self-regulating'. Even Socialists believed that the economy would regulate itself once private property had been abolished. The job of the nation state and of its government was seen as maintaining the 'climate' for economic growth and prosperity – by keeping the currency stable, taxes low, and by encouraging thrift and savings. Economic 'weather', that is, economic fluctuations, were beyond anyone's control – if only because the events causing these fluctuations were likely to be world-market events rather than events within the nation state itself.

The Great Depression gave rise to the belief that the national government is – and should be – in control of the economic weather. John Maynard Keynes (1883–1946) first asserted that the national economy is insulated from the world economy at least in medium-sized and large countries. Then he claimed that this insulated national economy is totally determined by government policy, i.e. by government spending. However much today's economists otherwise differ from Keynes, they all – Friedmanites. Supply-siders and the other Post-Keynesians – follow Keynes in these two tenets. They all make the nation state and its government the master of the national economy and the controller of its economic weather.

The Fiscal State

The two world wars of this century turned the national state into the 'Fiscal State'. Until World War I no government in history was ever able – not even in wartime – to obtain from its people more than a very small fraction of the country's national income, perhaps 5% or 6%. But in World War I every belligerent country, even the poorest, found that there was practically no limit to what government could squeeze out of the population. By World War I the economies of all belligerent countries were fully monetized. As a result, the two poorest countries, Austria-Hungary and Russia, could actually tax and borrow in several of the World War I years more than the total annual income of their respective populations. They managed to liquidate capital accumulated over long decades, if not over centuries, and turn it into war material.

Joseph Schumpeter, then still living in Austria, immediately understood what had happened. But the rest of the economists and most governments needed a second lesson – World War II. Since then, however, all developed – and many developing – countries have become 'Fiscal States'. They have all come to believe that there are no *economic* limits to what government can tax or borrow and, therefore, no economic limits to what government can spend.

What Schumpeter pointed out was that as long as governments have been around, the budget process has begun with an assessment of the available revenues. Expenditures then had to be fitted to these revenues. And since the supply of 'good causes' is inexhaustible, and the demand for spending therefore infinite, the budgeting process mostly consisted of deciding where to say 'no'. As long as revenues were known to be limited, governments, whether democracies or absolute monarchies like the Russian Tsar, operated under extreme restraints. These restraints made it impossible for government to be a social agency or to be an economic agency.

But since World War I – and even more since World War II – the budgeting process means, in effect, saying 'yes'.

Traditionally, government, the political society, had available only such means as the civil society granted it – and that only within the very narrow limits of a few per cent of national income, which is all that could be monetized. Only that amount could be converted into taxes and loans, and therefore into government revenues. Under the new dispensation, which assumes that there are no economic limits to the revenues it can obtain, government becomes the master of civil society and able to mould and shape it. By using taxes and expenditures government can, above all, redistribute society's income. Through the power of the purse it can, or so it was promised, shape society in the politician's image.

But also under the new dispensation it is only too easy to see national income as belonging to government with individuals entitled only to whatever government is willing to let them have. No one before 1914 – actually no one before 1946 – spoke of 'tax loopholes'. The assumption in earlier days was that everything belongs to the individual, unless it has been expressly conveyed to government by the taxpayers' political representatives, whether an absolute government or a parliament.

The term 'tax loophole', however, implies that everything belongs to government unless it has been especially designated to be retained by the taxpayer. And whatever taxpayers retain they do so only because government in its wisdom and generosity is willing to let them have it.

Of course, this became explicit only in the Communist countries. But even in the United States, especially during the Kennedy years, it was received wisdom in Washington and especially among the Washington bureaucracy that all income belongs to government except whatever government expressly and explicitly permits the taxpayer to keep.

The Cold-War State

The Welfare State; government as the master of the economy; and the Fiscal State – all grew out of social and economic problems and social and economic theories. The last of the mutations which created the Megastate, the Cold-War State, was a response to technology.

Its origin was the German decision, in the 1890s, to build in peacetime a massive naval deterrent. This started the armaments race. The Germans knew that they took an enormous political risk. In fact, most German politicians resisted the decision. But the German admirals were convinced that technology left them no choice. A modern navy meant steel-clad ships. And such ships had to be built in peacetime. To wait for the outbreak of war as traditional policy would have dictated would have meant waiting too long.

Since 1500 or so, when the knight had become obsolete, warfare increasingly was waged with weapons produced in ordinary peacetime facilities with a minimum of delay or adaptation. In the American Civil War cannons were still being produced in hastily adapted peacetime workshops and factories, and only after hostilities had broken out. Textile mills switched practically overnight from civilian clothing to uniforms. The two major wars fought during the second half of the nineteenth century, the American Civil War (1861-1865) and the Franco-Prussian War (1870-1871), were still largely waged by civilians who had put on the uniform only a few weeks before engaging in combat.

Modern technology, the German admirals of 1890 argued, had changed all this. The wartime economy could no longer be an adaptation of the peacetime economy. The two had to be separate. Both weapons and fighting men had to be available, and in large quantities, *before* the outbreak of hostilities. To produce either required increasingly long lead times.

Defence, it was implicit in the German argument, no longer meant keeping warfare away from civilian society and civilian economy. Under conditions of modern technology, defence means a permanent wartime society and a permanent wartime economy. It means the 'Cold-War State'.

The most astute political observer around the turn of the century, the French Socialist leader Jean Jaurès (1859–1914), understood this even before World War I. Woodrow Wilson (1856–1924) learned it from World War I; it underlay his proposal for a League of Nations, that is, for a permanent organization monitoring national armaments. The first attempt to use military build-ups as a means for arms control was the – abortive – Washington Naval Armaments Conference of 1923.

But even after World War II, the United States, for a few short years, tried to get back to a 'normal' peacetime state. It tried to disarm as fast as possible, and as completely as possible. The coming of the Cold War in the Truman and Eisenhower years changed all this. Since then the Cold-War State has been the dominant organization of international politics.

By 1960 the Megastate had become political reality in developed countries – in all its aspects; as social agency, as master of the economy; as Fiscal State – and in most countries as Cold-War State.

The Japanese exception

The one exception is Japan. Whatever the truth about 'Japan Inc.' – and there is little truth to what is commonly understood in the West by this term – the Japanese after World War II did not adopt the Cold-War State. Their government did not try to become the master of the economy. It did not try to become master of society. Rather, it rebuilt itself after the shattering defeat on what, in effect, were traditional nineteenth-century lines. Militarily, of course, Japan had no choice. But Japan instituted almost no social programmes. The only exception was national health insurance, largely imposed on it by the victorious Americans during the Occupation. Japan did not nationalize industries. In effect, Japan was the only developed country – until Margaret Thatcher's Britain began to 'privatize' industry in the 1980s – in which industries that had earlier become nationalized (e.g. the steel industry) were returned to private ownership.

Viewed through the glasses of traditional political theory, that is, of the political theory of the eighteenth and early nineteenth centuries, Japan is clearly a 'statist' country. But it is statist in the way in which Germany or France in 1880 or 1890 were 'statist' compared to Britain or the United States. It has a large civil service (though no larger proportionately than the civil services of the English-speaking countries). Government service enjoys tremendous prestige and respect, the way government service in 1890 Germany, 1890 Austria-Hungary or 1890 France enjoyed tremendous respect. Government in Japan works closely with big business – again no different from the way government in Continental Europe worked with economic interests in the late nineteenth century – and in fact not too different from the way American government worked with business or the farm interest around the turn of the century.

If the Megastate is taken as the norm – that is, if reality rather than theory is the basis for judging political systems – Japan since World War II has been the country in which government has played the most restricted and in fact the most restrained role. It is exceedingly powerful in traditional nineteenth-century terms. It is least prominent in the spheres into which twentieth-century government has moved in the rest of the world. Government in Japan is still primarily a guardian.*

For 30 years, from the end of World War II until the mid-1970s, the entire world moved towards the Megastate.

Japan has been the one exception. Elsewhere the movement towards the Megastate has been universal throughout the developed world. And the developing countries rapidly followed suit. No sooner was a new nation state formed out of the dissolution of an empire than it went into the new military policy, that is, into building in peacetime a wartime military establishment, and into building or at least procuring the advanced arms needed in case of war. It immediately tried to get control of society. It immediately tried to use the tax mechanism to redistribute income. And finally, almost without exception, it tried to become the manager and, in large part, also the owner of the economy.

As regards political freedom, intellectual freedom and religious

* In 1915 the brilliant American sociologist Thorstein Veblen (1857–1929) in a book entitled *Imperial Germany and the Industrial Revolution* tried to explain the rise of Germany to economic dominance. Two-thirds of a century later an American economist Chalmers Johnson, one of the country's leading experts on Japanese economic policy, tried similarly to explain the rise of Japan to economic great power status in a book entitled *Miti and the Japanese Miracle* (Stanford University Press, 1982). Johnson clearly believes Japanese economy policies in the post-World War II period to be of purely Japanese origin and invention. Yet the policies Veblen described as the reasons for Germany's almost explosive economic growth in the 40 years before World War I bear an uncanny resemblance to those Johnson describes.

freedom, the totalitarian countries (especially the Stalinist ones) and the 'democracies' (which for a good many years meant primarily the English-speaking countries) were total antitheses. But in terms of the underlying *theory* of government these systems differed more in degree than they did in kind. The democracies differed in how to do things. They differed far less in respect to what things should be done. They all saw government as the master of society and the master of the economy. And they all saw 'peace' as being 'Cold War'.

Has the Megastate worked?

Has the Megastate worked? In its most extreme manifestation, in totalitarianism, whether of the Nazi or of the Communist variety, it has surely been a total failure – without a single redeeming feature. It may be argued that the Cold-War State worked militarily for the Soviet Union. For 40 years it was a military superpower. But the economic and social burden of the military establishment was so great as to become unbearable. It certainly contributed, and heavily, to the collapse of Communism and of the Russian Empire altogether.

But has the Megastate worked in its much more moderate form? Has it worked in the developed countries of Western Europe and in the United States? The answer is: hardly any better. By and large, it has been almost as great a fiasco there as in Hitler's Germany or in Stalin's Russia.

The Megastate has been least successful as a Fiscal State. Nowhere has it succeeded in bringing about a meaningful redistribution of income. In fact, the past 40 years have amply confirmed Pareto's Law (named after the Swiss-Italian economist Vilfredo Pareto (1848–1923)), according to which income distribution between major classes in society is determined by two factors, and by two factors only: the culture of the society and the level of productivity within the economy. The more productive an economy, the greater the equality of income; the less productive, the greater the inequality of income. Taxes, Pareto's Law asserts, cannot change this. But the advocates of the Fiscal State based their case in large measure on the assertion that taxation could effectively and permanently change income distribution. All our experience of the last 40 years disproves this claim.

The clearest case is the Soviet Union. Officially dedicated to equality, it established a very large *nomenklatura* of privileged functionaries who enjoyed income levels way beyond anything even the rich enjoyed under the Tsar. The more Soviet productivity stagnated, the greater did income inequality become in the Soviet Union. But the United States is also a good example. As long as American productivity increased, that is, until the late 1960s or early 1970s, equality of income distribution increased steadily. While the rich were still getting richer, the poor were getting richer much faster, and the middle class got richer much faster still. As soon as the productivity increases dropped or disappeared – that is, beginning with the Vietnam War – income inequality began to increase steadily in the United States, regardless of taxation. It made little difference that in the Nixon and Carter years the rich were taxed heavily or that in the Reagan years they were taxed much more lightly. Similarly, in the United Kingdom, despite a professed commitment to egalitarianism, and despite a tax system designed to minimize income inequality, income distribution has become steadily less equal in the last 30 years as productivity stopped growing.

Despite all its corruptions and scandals, the most egalitarian country is now Japan – the country of the fastest productivity increases and the fewest attempts to redistribute income through taxation.

The other economic claim of the Megastate, and of modern economic theory, that the economy can be successfully managed if government controls substantial parts of the gross national income, has equally been disproven. The Anglo-American countries fully embraced this theory. Yet there has been no decline in the number, the severity or the length of their recessions. Recessions have been as numerous and have lasted just as long as they did in the nineteenth century. In the countries that did not embrace modern economic theory – and neither Japan nor Germay have – recessions have been less frequent, less severe and of shorter duration than in the countries that believe that the size of the government surplus or of the government deficit, that is, government spending, effectively manages the economy and can effectively smooth out cyclical fluctuations.*

* The one example always cited in support of modern economic theory and its claim to be able to control recessions, the so-called 'Kennedy tax cut' of the early 1960s in the United States, is a mirage. There was no such tax cut. Federal taxes

The one result of the Fiscal State is the opposite of what it aims at. Governments in all developed countries – and in most developing ones as well – have become such heavy spenders that they cannot increase their expenditures in a recession. But that is, of course, the time when, according to all modern economic theory, they should do so in order to create purchasing power and with it revive the economy. In every single developed country governments have reached the limits of their ability to tax and their ability to borrow. They have reached these limits during boom times, when they should, according to modern economic theory, build up sizable surpluses. The Fiscal State has spent itself into impotence.

Another basic tenet of the Fiscal State has also been shown to be invalid. Central to Keynesian and post-Keynesian economic theory is the belief that the total tax take is the one thing that matters. The last 40 years have proved that *what* is being taxed matters as much as *how much* is being taxed. What economists call the *incidence of taxation* is decisive – a notion that is dismissed rather contemptuously by post-World War II economists.* (On this, see also Chapter 8.)

The Pork-Barrel State

Worst of all, the Fiscal State has become the 'Pork-Barrel State'. If budget making starts with expenditures there is no fiscal discipline. Government spending becomes the means for politicians to buy votes. The strongest argument against the *Ancien Régime*, the eighteenth-century absolute monarchy, was that the king used the public purse to enrich his favourite courtiers. Fiscal accountability, and especially budget accountability to an elected legislature, was established to build accountability into government and to prevent courtiers from looting the commonwealth. In the Fiscal State the looting is done by politicians to ensure their own election.

were indeed cut. But at the same time, state and local governments increased their taxes beyond what the federal government cut so that the total tax burden actually increased – and despite this, the economy recovered, and recovered exactly according to the timetable on which it would have recovered without government intervention.

* The basic work on this was done long before World War I by the American economist Edward R. A. Seligman (1861–1939), especially in his 1892 classic *Shifting and Incidence of Taxation*.

An ever-larger share of US budgets – federal, state, municipal – is spent on subsidies for very small groups of local constituents: a handful of tobacco farmers in North Carolina; an even smaller number of peanut growers in Georgia; sugarcane growers in Louisiana; obsolescent industries in a mid-Western state; the wealthiest 5% of the retired Social Security recipients; the owners of land taken over for a canal or a dam which serves no economic purpose; or the small town next to an army base which has no military significance. What proportion of total government spending in the United States goes to favours for constituents which serve no public policy purpose – and which in many cases are totally at odds with public policy – nobody quite knows. But it is very high in both federal and state budgets – far higher than anyone realizes. In Japan the extent to which a politician's role is seen increasingly as diverting large sums from the public purse to small numbers of constituents has become a public scandal – to high-speed roads that lead nowhere, to subsidies to grow this or not to grow that, and so on.

The most brazen and gigantic pork-barrel vote buying occurred in Germany in the autumn of 1990, when Chancellor Helmut Kohl saddled his country with the biggest peacetime public debt ever taken on in order to buy – successfully – the votes of his new constituents in the former East Germany.

Democratic government rests on the belief that the first job of elected representatives is to defend their constituents against rapacious government. The Pork-Barrel State thus increasingly undermines the foundations of a free society. The elected representatives fleece their constituents to enrich special-interest groups and thereby to buy their votes. This is a denial of the concept of citizenship – and is beginning to be seen as such. That indeed it is undermining the very foundations of representative government is shown by the steady decline in voting participation. It is shown also by the steady decline in all countries of interest in the function of government, in issues, in policy. Instead voters increasingly vote on the basis of 'what's in it for me?'.

In 1918 Joseph Schumpeter warned that the Fiscal State would in the end undermine government's ability to govern. Fifteen years later Keynes hailed the Fiscal State as the great liberator: no longer limited by restraints on spending, government in the Fiscal State could now effectively govern. We now know that Schumpeter was right.

In the social sphere the Megastate has been somewhat more successful than in the economic one. Still, it has not even earned a passing grade. Or rather the social actions and policies that have worked well are those that, by and large, do not fit the doctrine of the Megastate. They are the social policies that follow earlier rules and earlier concepts. They are social policies that *regulate* or social policies that *provide*. They are not social policies in which government becomes the doer. Those, with few exceptions, have not been successful.

In the British National Health Service the part that *pays* general practitioners for patients on their lists works extremely well. But in the other part – where government manages hospitals and dispenses health care – there has been problem after problem. Costs are high and are going up as fast as health-care costs go up in any other country. Patients have to wait for years for elective surgery, that is, for the correction of conditions that are serious but not life threatening, whether a hip replacement, fixing a prolapsed uterus or removing a cataract in the eye. That during these months or years the patient is in pain and often disabled is irrelevant. As a doer, government has become so incompetent that the UK government is now encouraging hospitals to 'contract out' of the National Health Service. Government will pay hospitals as it does general practitioners but will no longer manage them.

Equally instructive are the American policies of the War on Poverty which President Johnson started with such good intentions in the 1960s. One of these programmes has worked. It is Headstart, which pays independent and locally managed organizations to teach disadvantaged – and primarily Black – pre-school children. None of the programmes government itself runs has, however, had results.

The most successful social policies of the last 10 or 15 years have been those in which governments – local governments primarily – 'contract out', either to a business or to a non-profit agency. The number of programmes successfully 'contracted out' is growing, and growing fast. Originally, services such as cleaning the streets were contracted out. But now the United States is contracting out social programmes like Headstart or the rehabilitation of youthful offenders. And, in the United States at least, we will increasingly contract out schooling. Increasingly, the United States is going in for 'vouchers' under which the parents can decide to which school, public or even private, they want to send their children, with the state paying to the school of the parent's choice. We are, in other words, beginning to apply to elementary education what we learned 40 years ago in the GI Bill of Rights in respect to higher education. Government sets the rules, government sets the standards, government provides. But government does not *do*.

The Cold-War State: failure of success

The Cold-War State did not guarantee 'peace'. During the post-World War II years there were as many 'minor' conflicts as in any period of history – and all over the world. But the Cold-War State made possible the avoidance of major global war, not despite the tremendous military arsenal but because of it.

The arms race made possible arms control. This resulted in the longest period without great-power war in modern history. Fifty years have now gone by without military conflict between great powers. The peace settlement of the Congress of Vienna after the Napoleonic Wars – so celebrated by present-day *Realpoliticians* like Henry Kissinger – maintained great-power peace for 38 years, from 1815 until the outbreak of the Crimean War in 1853. Then, after almost 20 years of major conflicts – the American Civil War, the war between Prussia and Austria, the war between France and Germany – there were 43 years, from 1871 to 1914, in which no great power fought another (except for the war between Japan and Russia in 1905 – but then Japan was not considered a great power until after that war). Only 21 years elapsed between World War I and World War II. The near-50 years following 1945 in which no great power fought another great power is thus a record. Precisely because they had become Cold-War States the major powers could control armaments and could thereby make sure that there was no such preponderance of military might as would tempt one of them to risk major conflict.

The best example is the Cuban Missile Crisis. This was largely caused by President Kennedy's blunder in not standing up to Russia over the Berlin Wall and by his misjudgement and vacillation during the Bay of Pigs invasion of Cuba. This convinced Khrushchev that the United States would buckle down and accept the establishment of a Russian nuclear base in the Western

Hemisphere. As soon, however, as it became clear that the United States would not tolerate such provocation, the Russians retracted – and because Khrushchev had carelessly misjudged and thereby risked a major conflict with another great power, he was soon overthrown by his own military.

The 50 years since the end of World War II have fully proven the basic assumptions on which the Cold-War State has been based. The weapons of modern war can no longer be produced in facilities that also produce the goods needed for peacetime. They cannot be produced by converting civilian facilities to wartime production, as was still largely done in World War II. In turn, the facilities that produce the weapons of modern war, whether an aircraft carrier, a 'smart bomb' or a guided missile, have to be built long before there is a war or even the threat of one.

If any proof of these assumptions had been needed, the 1991 war against Iraq provided it. None of the weapons which paralysed what was one of the world's largest military forces, and which decided a war in the shortest time in which any war had ever been decided before (breaking the record established in 1866, when the Prussians knocked out the Austrians in four weeks), could have been produced in any peacetime facility. Each weapons system had required at least 10 and in most cases 15 years of work before it could become effective on the battlefield.

There is no going back, therefore, to the assumptions on which the traditional nation state had been founded: a small military force augmented by reservists is all that is needed to hold the field while civilian economic facilities are being converted to wartime production.

But the 50 years during which the Cold-War State worked are also over. We need arms control more than ever. There is no return to 'peace' if defined as the absence of military might. Innocence, once lost, can never be recovered. But the Cold-War State is no longer tenable. It no longer works.

The Cold-War State has become economically self-destructive. The Soviet Union, as already said, succeeded in building an exceedingly powerful military force. But the burden this military force imposed became so intolerably heavy that it played a major part in the collapse of Soviet economy and Soviet society.

The burden is becoming equally heavy for the United States. As is now generally accepted, one of the main reasons Japan and Germany have economically been doing so well while the United

States has been falling behind is US defence. The economic burden – 5% or 6% of GNP – is the lesser problem. It is the diversion of the scarcest resources – trained engineers and scientists – to economically unproductive defence work. In the United States 70% of all money spent on research and development is spent on defence work. In Japan it is less than 5%. This conceals an even more important qualitative difference. Defence research in the United States has attracted the best and brightest of young engineers and scientists, thus starving the American economy of the most needed nourishment, that is, of knowledge. Where the ablest American engineers these last 40 years have worked on 'smart bombs', their Japanese counterparts have worked on perfecting the fax machine or on taking the rattle out of a car door. Peacetime goods and wartime goods are no longer being produced by the same technologies, by the same processes and in the same facilities. There is therefore no longer much, if any, 'fallout'. The United States has spent enormous sums of money on 'technology transfer' from defence research to civilian products. The results have been close to zero.

Even worse were the effects of the Cold-War State on economic development. There is very little doubt that Latin America rather than East Asia would have been the 'economic miracle' of the 1960s and 1970s but for the fact that money and trained people in those countries were wasted on building huge armed forces without any military value.

A nation – even the richest – that spends in peacetime more than 2% or 2½% of its GNP on armaments – still twice as much as Japan spends – cannot expect for very long to remain competitive in the world economy. It will be under increasing inflationary pressure. In fact it should be considered as *not creditworthy*.

But even militarily the Cold-War State no longer works. In fact the Cold-War State can no longer guarantee arms control. There is no way anymore to maintain the 'superpower monopoly' in such a way that smaller nations will be prevented from building total-war capacity, whether nuclear or chemical or biological. Worry over control of the Soviet Union's nuclear arsenal as the empire disintegrates into individual nation states is just one indication. So is the fact that any number of countries that are otherwise quite insignificant in terms of population or economic strength are rapidly acquiring nuclear, chemical and biological warfare capacity – Iraq was one example, Libya is another and so are Iran,

North Korea and Pakistan. These small countries could not, of course, win a war against a great power – as Iraq's Saddam Hussein still believed. But they can become international black-mailers and international terrorists. With such countries as their base small bands of adventurers – land-based pirates, in effect – can hold the world to ransom.

Arms control can thus no longer be exercised in and through the Cold-War State as it was for the half-century after World War II. Unless arms control becomes transnational, it cannot be exercised at all – which would make global conflict practically inevitable even if the major powers still manage to avoid Hot War between themselves.

Unlike Fiscal State and Nanny State, the Cold-War State has not been a total failure. Insofar as the aim of national policy in the age of the absolute weapons can be said to be the avoidance of World War III, it must be considered a success – the only success of the Megastate. But in the end this success turned to failure – economically and militarily.

The Megastate has thus reached a dead end. But, alas, there is no going back to yesterday's nation state, as neo-conservatives or economists of the Austrian School would make us believe. For there are new forces arising which both outflank and undermine the nation state.

7

Transnationalism, regionalism, tribalism

Even before World War I, politicians and political scientists warned that the nation state was becoming outmoded and called for supernational institutions. In fact the nineteenth century had already created quite a few. The treaties of earlier centuries had been between one state and another. The nineteenth century wrote multinational treaties – one after the other. The first half of the century produced multinational conventions to stamp out piracy and the slave trade and to guarantee the freedom of the seas. The multinational treaties of the nineteenth century's second half, e.g. the International Postal Union and the International Red Cross, for the first time set up non-national and, indeed, supernational agencies. In the early years of the twentieth century the International Court of Justice in The Hague was established and given jurisdiction over disputes between national states. These non-national or transnational treaties and agencies were, however, seen as dealing with 'technical' matters and thus not infringing on national sovereignty. (That was surely fiction though. The International Red Cross was given the right of inspection of prisoner-of-war camps in wartime; The Hague Court was given jurisdiction over boundary disputes between national states.)

After World War I it became conventional wisdom that the nation state was obsolete. This belief underlay the attempt to create the first avowedly supernational agency, the League of Nations. But it proved impotent right away. And for its first 40 years the United Nations, set up after World War II, served primarily as an arena in which the superpowers fought each other. A post-World War II attempt to create a transnational currency was sponsored by John Maynard Keynes in the last months of his life. It was defeated by the Americans. In turn, the American proposal to transnationalize the atom – the Baruch Plan for transnational control of nuclear energy and nuclear arms – was rejected by the Russians. And the most successful of these post-World War II inventions, GATT (the General Agreement on Tariffs and Trade), while clearly meant to impose transnationalism in an area central to sovereignty (i.e. foreign trade) has rarely prevailed against national interests.

Instead, the period after World War II saw both explosive growth in the number of nation states as the successors to the prewar empires all organized themselves as such and the mutation of the nation state into the Megastate.

But in the last decades – beginning perhaps in the 1970s – the nation state began to come apart. It has already been *outflanked* in crucial areas where sovereignty has lost all meaning. Increasingly, the new challenges facing every government are challenges that simply cannot be dealt with by national or even international action. They require *transnational agencies* who have 'sovereignty' of their own. Increasingly, *regionalism* is also sidelining the nation state. And internally, the nation state is being undermined by *tribalism*.

Money knows no fatherland

'Money knows no fatherland' is a very old saying. But the nation state was invented in large part to disprove it. Control over money was at the very centre of what came to be called 'sovereignty'. But money has slipped the leash. It has gone transnational. It cannot be controlled any longer by national states, and not even by their acting together.

No central bank any longer controls money flows. It can try to influence them by raising or lowering interest rates. But in the flow of money political factors are increasingly as important as interest rates. The amount of money beyond the control of any one central bank, that is, the amount traded every day on the transnational markets – the New York Foreign Exchange Market or the London Interbank Market – so greatly exceeds anything needed to finance national and international transactions that the flows escape any attempt to control them, to limit them, let alone to manage them.

Nor does information

Information was not included in Bodin's attributes of sovereignty – there was not much of it in the late 1500s. But when mass media emerged in this century – print, films or radio – control of information was at once seen as essential by the new practitioners of national sovereignty, the totalitarians. Beginning with Lenin, every one of them – Mussolini, Stalin, Hitler – tried to exercise total control over information. And in the democratic countries mastery of information – especially of television – increasingly became the central art of politicians and politics.

By now, information has gone transnational fully as much as has money. Governments can still control the news programmes. But even in Germany during World War II as many people clandestinely listened to the BBC as listened to Nazi propaganda chief Joseph Goebbels on the evening news. But news programmes are an increasingly small part of 'information'. Any 30-second advertisement, any 18-minute soap-opera episode contains as much information as the most carefully controlled news programme – maybe more. There are no national boundaries anymore for information. Surely the increasing inability of the most absolute regime in history to control access to information was a major factor in the collapse of Communism and of the Soviet Empire.

Information may be distorted; the picture of American life conveyed by one of the world's most popular television programmes, *Dallas*, is not even a caricature. But that does not alter the fact that *Dallas* has been seen by more people in more countries than any other kind of 'message'. Even in Communist China it could not be kept off the air. In a few years, with receiving 'dishes' so small that no secret police can prevent their use inside the home, and with satellites overhead beaming programmes to any point of the globe, information, for better or worse, will have become truly transnational and truly beyond the control of any one country. Countries concerned about the integrity of their own national culture (e.g. Japan or France) will attempt to protect sovereign control of popular information. But such attempts are futile, as has been abundantly proven.

It *may* be possible to restore control over money through a transnational institution. The European Community is moving towards a European Central Bank and a European common currency. But this would be tantamount to transnational control of economic and tax policy. It would reduce the national state in the economic sphere to the position of a local administrator. In respect to information, no such transnational institution is even possible – not even under a world dictatorship. Modern technology endows the individual with the means to circumvent totalitarian controls on information. Banning fax machines and copying machines was still attempted by the Communists in their last desperate attempt to maintain control of information. It only led to underground publications, the *samizdat*, the manuscripts copied by hand by hundreds or thousands of students and circulating freely throughout the Soviet Union. Once people have laptop computers, fax machines, telephones, copiers, videocassette recorders, in their possession and in their homes – let alone television receivers which can pluck messages from any satellite overhead – there is no way to re-establish control over information.

Money going transnational outflanks the nation state by nullifying national economic policy. Information going transnational outflanks the nation state by undermining – in fact destroying – the identification of 'national' with 'cultural' identity. What does it mean to be a 'Frenchman' if most of them prefer Charlie Chaplin to any play written by a French writer and produced in France? a 1920 critic asked when films first made their appearance. But now French – and Americans, English, Germans, Russians, Japanese and Chinese – prefer Charlie Chaplin's successors, the situation comedies or the 'docudramas' to anything produced in their own country. 'High culture' has gone supernational fully as much as 'popular culture'. Architecture surely conveys are much of a 'message' as does a TV show or a news bulletin; and there is little difference between the office buildings that go up in Tokyo and those that go up in Dallas or in Duesseldorf.

The transnational needs: the environment

Fully as important – indeed more important in the long run – are the growing needs for truly transnational institutions, that is, for institutions that in their own sphere transcend the nation state. These institutions can – indeed they must – make decisions and take actions in a wide range of areas which cut through the barrier of sovereignty and directly control citizens and organizations within a nation state. These decisions push aside the nation state or turn it into an agent of the transnational institution.

The first of these areas is the *environment*. Local *action* is needed to prevent destructive pollution. But the biggest threat to the environment is not local pollution, whether the effluents of a paper mill, the wastes spewed into the oceans by municipal sewage or the runoff of pesticides and fertilizers from local farms. The damage is to the human habitat, to the atmosphere, to the tropical forests which are, so to speak, the Earth's lungs, to the Earth's oceans, to its water supply and to the air – the environment on which all of humanity depends. But there is also the need to balance protection of the environment and the demands of the developing world with its rapidly growing population.

These are not challenges which can be tackled within the borders of a national state. Pollution knows no boundaries any more than do money or information.

The forests of Scandinavia, which may be Europe's greatest natural resource, are being destroyed by pollution generated in the English Midlands and in Scotland, in Belgium and in Germany. Acid rain which similarly threatens the forests of Canada – maybe the greatest natural resource of North America – is generated in the American Midwest.

But maintaining the Amazonian rain forest in effect means putting severe short-term limitations on the ability of a growing Brazilian population to feed itself. Who will pay for this, and how?

Stamping out terrorism

Second only to the environment is the growing need for transnational action and transnational institutions to abort the return of private armies, that is, to stamp out terrorism. The military action against Iraq in the winter and spring of 1991 may have been the starting point. For the first time in recorded history practically all the nation states acted together to put down an act of terrorism – for this is what the Iraqi invasion of Kuwait represented.

For the first time in 400 years, private armies have returned. In the seventeenth century Japan (around 1600) and Europe 50 years later decided that the nation state alone could be allowed to maintain a military force. But with nuclear explosives, chemical weapons and biological weapons, private armies have again become possible. Terrorism is all the more threatening as very small groups can effectively hold even large countries to hostage. A nuclear bomb can easily be put into a locker or a post box in any major city and be exploded by remote control – and so could a bacterial bomb containing enough anthrax spores to kill thousands of people and to contaminate a big city's water supply and make it uninhabitable.

Twenty years ago many countries, especially the Communist ones, thought that terrorism could be used as a tool of national policy. There is little doubt, for instance, that the terrorist groups in West Germany were recruited, financed and trained in East Germany. There is little doubt that Iraq, Iran, Syria and Libya all recruited, financed and trained terrorist groups – for instance, the Japanese Red Army faction – to terrorize the Western world and especially the United States.

By now most countries – though by no means all – have realized that this is counterproductive. But not to support terrorism is not enough. What is needed to eliminate – or at least to control – the threat of terrorism is transnational action, action that goes beyond any one sovereign state. There is a precedent: the nineteenth-century treaties which stamped out the slave trade and made piracy on the high seas a transnational offence.

Transnational arms control

Third – and closely connected with the stamping out of terrorism – is the need for transnational arms control – the need discussed in the previous chapter.

Finally – so far, still speculation – will there be a transnational agency to monitor and to enforce human rights? Should there be such an agency? Would such an agency, for instance, have been able to prevent Hitler's Holocaust? Jimmy Carter clearly favoured such an agency while US President in the 1970s. What might actually bring it about is the threat to prosperous countries of being inundated by millions of refugees unless transnational action stops racial, religious, political and ethnic persecution.

We may already have moved further towards transnationalism than most of us – and especially most politicians – realize. In respect to the environment, we are close to transnational action to prevent, or at least to slow down, ozone depletion and the 'greenhouse effect', that is, worldwide warming. We are close to transnational action to protect the oceans and their resources. There already is a multilateral treaty to protect Antarctica.

In respect to terrorism and arms control the turning point may indeed have been the Iraqi War, and especially the decision to entrust the destruction of Iraq's terror weapons – nuclear, chemical and biological – to agencies of the United Nations rather than to have this task carried out by an army under US command. Even earlier, in a step that was totally unprecedented – and indeed ran counter to all earlier American legal principles – the US Government proposed an International Criminal Court with direct jurisdiction over acts of terrorism committed anywhere. And the new government of the Russian Republic has revived the original Baruch Plan of 1947 and has proposed to hand over control of all nuclear weapons worldwide to a transnational agency – which, in effect, would then result in the elimination of all nuclear weapons worldwide and in transnational action to stop any attempt by any country to build nuclear arms facilities.

The design of the needed transnational agencies is still ahead of us. So is the speed with which any of them will develop. It may well take major catastrophes to make national governments willing to accept subordination to such transnational institutions and their decisions. The development of such institutions, the decision as to the spheres in which they act, their constitution, their power, their relationship to national governments, their financing (should they, for instance, have taxing power of their own?) are still well ahead of us. We are indeed completely unprepared – as witness the ludicrous wrangling over who should pay what share of the costs of the military action in Iraq in 1991. But it is predictable that the design and construction of transnational institutions will be central political issues for many decades to come. This means that the *limitation of sovereignty* will become a central issue in international relations and in foreign as well as in domestic politics.

The new reality: regionalism

Internationalism is no longer Utopia; it is already on the horizon – but barely so. *Regionalism* is reality: regionalism does not create a superstate whose government *replaces* national government. It creates regional governing agencies that sideline national government in important areas and make it increasingly irrelevant.

The trend towards regionalism was triggered by the European Community. But it will not be confined to it. The European Community started out as a 'common market', that is, as a purely economic organization. It has assumed more and more political functions. It is on the point of creating a European Central Bank and a European currency. But it also has taken jurisdiction over access to trades and professions: over mergers, acquisitions and cartels; over social legislation; over everything that can possibly be construed as 'non-tariff barriers' to the free movement of goods, services and people. It is moving towards a European army.

The European Community then triggered the attempt to create a North American economic community built around the United States but integrating both Canada and Mexico into a common market. So far this attempt is purely economic in its goal. But it hardly can remain so in the long run.

What makes this so important is that the impetus for the North American economic community did not come from the United States. It came from Mexico. Yet for over 150 years, ever since Mexico was unified in the presidency of Benito Juarez (1806-1872), the goal of Mexican policy has been to put as much distance as possible between its country and its big pushy and totally alien neighbour to the north. No two contiguous countries in the world are as different as Mexico and the United States, in language, in religion, but above all in culture, in values, in tradition. Yet Mexico had to accept in the end that the 150 years of isolationist policy had ended in failure; in order to survive as a country and civilization it has to integrate itself with the big, dangerous and alien neighbour to the north, at least economically.

The treaty which the Mexican government has proposed to establish a customs union between Mexico and the other two North American countries, the United States and Canada, may fail to go through. But the economic integration of the three countries into one region is proceeding so fast that it will make little difference whether the marriage is sanctified legally or not.

The same will increasingly be true in East Asia. The only question is whether there will be one or several such economic regions. There might be a region in which coastal China and the countries of South-east Asia coalesce around Japan. It is possible also that rapidly growing coastal China which embraces about two-fifths of China's population and produces about two-thirds of China's National Product – from Tsientin in the north to Canton in the south – will establish itself as one region, with a Japan-oriented South-east Asia as a second region.

Which way Asia will go will be among the key questions in the 1990s and in the early years of the twenty-first century.

There is also a growing movement towards 'mini-regions'. No sooner did the Soviet Empire disintegrate than the 'Turkic' successor states in Central Asia proposed a 'Turkic Region' centred in the most Westernized and most highly developed Turkic country, i.e. Turkey. No sooner did the three Baltic countries, Lithuania, Latvia and Estonia, secede from the Soviet Empire than they began to talk of a 'Baltic Region' in which they would join with their Scandinavian neighbours – and above all with Finland and Sweden. A similar mini-region embracing the peoples and nations of South-east Asia – Malaysia, Singapore, Indonesia, the Philippines, Thailand – has been proposed by the prime minister of Malaysia. And an economic region replacing the old Soviet Union is what Russia's prime minister is pushing and hoping for.

But whether there are three or four or more such regions is less important than that the thrust towards regionalism is irreversible. It is also inevitable. It responds to the new economic reality. In the knowledge economy neither traditional protectionism nor traditional free trade can work by themselves. What is needed is an economic unit that is big enough to establish meaningful free trade and strong competition within the unit. This unit has to be large enough to allow new 'high-tech' industries to develop with a high degree of protection. The reason for this lies in the nature of high-tech, that is, of knowledge industry.

High-tech industry does not follow the supply-demand equations of classical, neo-classical and Keynesian economics. In those the costs of production go up proportionally to the volume of production. In high-tech industries the costs of production go *down* and very fast, as the volume of production goes up – what is now called the 'learning curve'. (For further discussion see Chapter 10.)

The significance of this is that a high-tech industry can establish itself in such a way that it will destroy any competitor – what I once called 'adversarial trade'. Once this has happened there is almost no chance for the defeated industry to come back. It has ceased to exist. At the same time, however, the new high-tech industry has to have enough competition and enough challenge – or else it will simply not grow and develop. It will become monopolistic and lazy and will soon be obsolete. The knowledge economy requires, therefore, economic units that are substantially *larger* than even a fair-sized national state. Otherwise there will be no competition. But it also requires the ability to protect industry and to conduct trade with other trading blocs on the basis of reciprocity rather than either protection or free trade. This is an unprecedented situation. It makes regionalism both inevitable and irreversible.

But regionalism, as the example of the European Community shows, is not simply 'international'. It has to establish transnational, indeed supernational, institutions.

The various regions as they are emerging are quite dissimilar. The European Community is built around a fairly small number of countries: Britain, Germany, France, Italy and Spain, which are roughly comparable in size and population, and which, despite great differences in wealth, are still ranged along a continuum of economic development. The most advanced Spanish company, for instance, is actually more advanced than the average German company.

The North American economic community would be very different. In population its three partners range from 250 million people in the United States to one-tenth that number in Canada. The three differ widely in economic development. Parts of the United States are the world's wealthiest areas. Parts of Mexico – especially the south – are among the world's poorest and least developed areas.

The economic regions in Asia will be even more different. They even will not all share a common cultural heritage – Indonesia or Malaysia never were part of Confucian culture.

But they will all create large free-trade areas, larger than free-trade areas have ever been before. At the same time, they will create large areas that are unified in their response to the outside world and capable of being 'reciprocal', that is, of being, at the same time, both wide open and protectionst.

These regions do not replace the nation state. But they sideline it.

The return of tribalism

Internationalism and regionalism challenge the sovereign nation state from the outside. Tribalism undermines it from within. It saps the nation state's integrating power. In fact, it threatens to replace nation by tribe.

In the United States, tribalism manifests itself in the growing emphasis on diversity rather than on unity. The United States has always been a country of immigrants. Every immigrant group was at first considered 'foreign' and was discriminated against until two generations later it had become 'mainstream' – beginning with the Irish in the 1830s and the 1840s. America was a 'melting pot'. In the last 30 years this has become highly unfashionable. Now diversity is preached and practised. Any attempt to make new groups into 'Americans' is considered 'discrimination' – only 60 years ago the attempt to *prevent* such groups from becoming 'Americans' would have been discrimination. Whether the new groups are Europeans or Asians, whether they are Black, Brown, or White, whether they are Catholics or Buddhists, the emphasis is now on maintaining their identity and of preventing their being encouraged, let alone forced, to become 'Americans'.

This is by no means an American phenomenon and cannot even be explained in purely American terms (though clearly, as in everything in American society, the basic American problem, that is, race relations between White and Black, is central to the phenomenon). Tribalism is even more rampant in Europe. It has torn asunder Yugoslavia in bloody civil war. It threatens civil war all over the former Russian Empire. Scots want to secede from the United Kingdom. Slovaks demand autonomy and separation from the Czechs. Belgium is torn by strife between Flemish and French-speaking Walloons. Tiny local groups, though never discriminated against, demand 'cultural autonomy' – e.g. the 150 000

Sorbs living in the woods south of Berlin who are the last survivors of the Slavic tribes that inhabited northern Germany more
than a thousand years ago.

Tribalism has become worldwide. Will Canada survive this cen-
tury? Or will it split into two parts, an English-speaking and a
French-speaking one? Or even into four parts: a French-speaking
Quebec; an English-speaking Ontario and Manitoba; the Prairie
Provinces; and British Columbia? (Where then would the
Maritimes go? And Newfoundland?) Will India remain united
politically? Will Corsica and Britanny stay within France? Will the
Lapps in northern Finland and northern Sweden gain autonomy?
Will Mexico stay united – or will the Indian south break away
from the Hispanic north? The list is endless.

One reason for the trend towards tribalism is that bigness no
longer confers much advantage. In the age of nuclear war, not
even the biggest country can defend its citizens. The smallest one
– Israel is a case in point – can build terror weapons.

With money and information having become transnational,
even very small units have become economically viable. Big or
small, everyone has equal access to money and information and
on the same terms. Indeed the true 'success stories' of the last 30
years have been very small countries.

In the 1920s the Austrian Republic, the remnant of the old
Austro-Hungarian Empire, was universally considered much
too small to be economically viable with fewer than 6 million
inhabitants. In fact, this was the main argument in favour of
Hitler's annexation of the country in Austria itself. The Austria
of the 1920s and 1930s was indeed in pitiful economic shape,
with chronic unemployment of up to 20%. Post-World War II
Austria is hardly larger. In addition, it had lost the trading area it
still had in the 1920s, the successor states to the former Austria-
Hungary. These countries had all become Communist. Yet post-
World War II Austria became one of Europe's most prosperous
countries.

So has Finland – equally small – or Sweden or Switzerland.
Hong Kong and Singapore have done even better. Twenty years
ago the most fervent nationalists in the three Baltic countries
which Stalin had annexed in 1940 did not believe that their country could survive economically on its own; now few doubt it. And
the same is true of Canadian Quebec.

After all, a small country can now join an economic region and thus get the best of two worlds: cultural and political independence and economic integration. It is surely no coincidence that tiny Luxembourg has been the most fervent 'European' of them all.

The need for roots

The main reason for tribalism is neither politics nor economics. It is existential. People need roots in a transnational world; they need community.

All educated people in Spain know Castilian (which the outside world calls Spanish). But the language many Spaniards increasingly speak in school and at home, and even in the office is Catalan or Basque or Galician or Andalusian. The change may be a change in emphasis. But it does represent a fundamental change in identity. Catalans, Basques, Galicians, Andalusians, see the same soap operas on their TV set. The products they buy are as likely to have been made in Japan or in the United States as in Spain. Increasingly, they work for an employer whose headquarters are in Tokyo, in South Korea, in New York, or in Dusseldorf. They live increasingly in a non-national and increasingly a transnational world. But they need local roots, they need to belong to a local community.

Tribalism is not the opposite of transnationalism; it is its *pole*. More and more American Jews marry outside their faith; but this is then the reason why they emphasize their Jewish roots and the culture of Judaism. In the 40 years since World War II there have been more and more Serb men who married Croatian women – and, conversely, more and more Serb women who married Bosnian Moslems or Croatians. But this only made the rest of the Serbs, Croats and Bosnians more conscious of their tribal identities. Welsh and Irish marry more and more English men and women, only to become more conscious of being Welsh and Irish. Tribalism thrives precisely because people increasingly realize that what happens in Osaka affects people in Slovenia who have no idea where Osaka is and can hardly find it on the map. Precisely because the world has become transnational in so many ways – and must become ever more transnational – people need to define themselves in terms they can understand. They need a geographic, a linguistic, a religious, a cultural, community which is visible to them and which, to use an old cliché: they can 'get their arms around'.

The Sorbs in the woods outside of Berlin do not cease to be part of Germany and part of German culture. But they also see themselves – and demand to be seen – as something distinct. The Latin American immigrants into Los Angeles – whether from Mexico or from Central America – become American citizens as soon as they possibly can. They expect to have the same opportunities as native-born Americans. They expect their children to have the same access to education, to careers, to jobs. But they also expect to be able to maintain Hispanic identity, Hispanic culture, Hispanic community. The more transnational the world becomes, the more tribal it will therefore also be.

This increasingly undermines the very foundations of the nation state. Indeed, it ceases to be a 'nation state' and becomes a 'state' plain and simple, that is, an administrative rather than a political unit.

Internationalism, regionalism, tribalism are rapidly creating a new polity, a new and complex political structure, and one without precedent. To use a mathematical metaphor, the post-capitalist polity has three vectors, each pulling in a different direction.

In the meantime as the old English saying has it, 'the work of government must go on'. The only institutions we have so far for this work are those of the nation state and its government. The first political task of the post-capitalist polity must be to restore the performance capacity of government which the Megastate has so seriously diminished.

8

The needed government turnaround

The next decades will make unprecedented demands on political courage, political imagination, political innovation, political leadership. They will demand high government competence. The demands will be *external* ones as well as *internal* ones.

Externally there is need for new thinking and radical innovations in several areas: the relationship between national government and transnational tasks, the relationship between national governments and regional organizations; and the relationship between new but also very different regions. The next decades should – and for the first time – see the emergence of political institutions transcending the nation state, and of supernational, indeed transnational, law. The designers and builders of these new institutions, and the drafters of this transnational law, will have to be national governments and national politicians.

Internally there is an equally demanding and equally urgent need to make government effective again – despite the transformation of society into a pluralism of organizations, and despite the near-collapse of government's capacity to make decisions under the pressure of special-interest groups and the 'tyranny of the small minority'.

The great fear of the eighteenth-century political thinkers – e.g.
the framers of the American Constitution – was the fear of 'factions', that is, of special-interest groups with their tendency to
make their own interest or issue a 'moral imperative' to which
everything else is subordinated. The brilliant answer to this fear
was the *Party*. It was invented simultaneously though indepen-
dently, in Britain, the United States and France in the two decades
between 1815 and 1835 in which so much of the modern world
came into being. The Party transcended faction. In Europe it was
organized around a vague ideology, a 'programme'. In the United
States it was organized around equally broad and vague 'interests'. But whatever its professed rationale, it was organized for a
common purpose: to gain and to hold political power. It was organized to *govern*. It therefore had to attract the voters 'in the middle'. It had to eschew extremes and had to be willing to
compromise. It had to confine its actions, when in power, to measures that would command support way beyond its own adher-
ents, that is, to actions that would be acceptable to that part of the
'middle' that had not voted for it. The clearest expression of this
principle is the provision in the American Constitution regarding
the Presidential veto; it can only be over-ridden by two-thirds of
both houses of the Congress. This means that it can be over-
ridden only if substantial members of both parties agree on a
measure. This forces both Congress and President to stay in the
middle.

But now the parties are in tatters everywhere. The ideologies
that enabled European parties to bring together disparate factions
into one organization to gain and control power have lost most of
their integrating power. The parties and their slogans make no
sense to voters, especially to younger ones. The traditional interest groups of the United States are largely gone; where are the
farmers, the workers, the small businessmen, on whom Mark
Hanna based the Republican Party in 1896 and who were then
taken over in 1932 by Franklin D. Roosevelt to forge the new
Democratic Party?

Governments have thus become powerless against the
onslaught of special-interest groups, have indeed become powerless to govern, that is, to make decisions and to enforce them.

It has become fashionable these last years to be 'anti-government'. But this won't work. We need strong, effective government. In fact, we can expect more rather than less government in

the next decades. The new tasks – protection of the environment; stamping out private armies and international terrorism; making arms control effective – all require more rather than less government. *But they require a different government.*

In the last 15 to 20 years one political leader after the other has come into power to 'cut back government' or to 'fight the insiders'. The first to be elected on such a platform was Jimmy Carter in the United States – followed by Ronald Reagan, who in turn was followed by another 'anti-government' candidate, George Bush. In the UK Margaret Thatcher was elected on an 'anti-government' platform and governed on it for ten years. The results have been pitiful. Government expenditures and government regulations have increased faster than ever before under these anti-government leaders. Spending under them has become totally out of control. And the more these governments spent, the less competent and less potent they became. Government did not 'grow'. It became obese and paralysed by its own overweight. No administration in American history has run a large deficit than that of President Bush. According to accepted wisdom, that should have made impossible any kind of recession. But the enormous jumps in government spending and government deficits during the first three years of the Bush Administration brought about the deepest and longest recession the United States suffered since World War II. Prime minister Thatcher – arguably the ablest and surely the most determined political leader of the Free World since General de Gaulle – similarly had little to show but growing deficits for her attempts to cut government back, to make it more effective and competent, and to turn around the British economy.

This is just as true in respect to France. President Mitterand dramatically increased French government expenditures – without achieving any results. Under his presidency France has steadily lost ground as an economic and industrial power. In Japan the very ability to govern is being undermined by the perpetual scandals which are the direct result of the Pork-Barrel State.

Yet only national governments and only their political leaders can do the jobs that have to be done. They alone have *legitimacy.*

Government therefore has to regain a modicum of performance capacity. It has to be *turned around.* The term itself is a business term. But to turn around any institution, whether a business, a union, a university, a hospital or a government, requires always the same three steps:

1. Abandonment of the things that do not work, the things that have never worked; the things that have outlived their usefulness and their capacity to contribute;
2. Concentration on the things that work, the things that do produce results, the things that improve the organization's ability to perform. This requires doing more of the things that have proven successful.
3. Analysis of the half-successes, half-failures. A turnaround requires abandonment of whatever in such areas does not perform and doing more of whatever does.

The futility of military aid

If one were to rank the policies of the Megastate in order of their futility, military aid would surely be at the top of things that have never worked, and therefore first on the list of things to abandon. Military aid goes back to hoary antiquity. Roman historians already pointed out that the military aid the King of Persia gave to Sparta in its war against Athens only made it possible, a few decades later, for the Macedonians to gain domination over Greece and thus to give Alexander the Great the army and the arms to overthrow the Persian Empire.

But surely military aid has never been used more extensively – and more unsuccessfully – than in the years of the Megastate, the years since World War II. It has backfired – practically without exception. Examples are the military aid the United States gave Iran under the Shah; the military aid the Soviet Union gave to Afghanistan; the military aid the United States gave to Iraq. Nor has the military aid given to any number of Latin-American generals been any more productive. It only made the generals rich and their countries poor.

To support a country that is under attack by a powerful enemy is one thing. To give military aid to 'friendly' regimes is another. It is extortion money – and that only increases the extortionist's appetite. To the threat: if you do not give us these planes, these tanks, these missiles, we'll get them elsewhere, the proper answer is: 'Go ahead.' And the oft-invoked need to maintain a 'military balance' in a region is pure sham. In no instance has military aid during the last 40 years stabilized a region. It has only stepped up the arms race.

Economic aid has been hotly debated these last years. Has it actually aided the recipients or has it weakened them? There is substance to the charge that food aid such as the United States has provided in huge quantities has allowed governments – especially in Africa – to neglect their own agriculture and to impoverish their own farmers. Altogether, government-to-government aid, that invention of the 1950s, has had, at best, marginal results. Not much more can be said for grants or loans made by or through quasi-governmental institutions such as the World Bank; few of them have provided substantial development. Still, the idea of economic aid may be a good one – though we obviously do not know how to do it.

But the idea of military aid is in itself a poor one. Military aid does not create reliable allies. In all probability aid recipients turn against the aid giver – as Iran and Iraq turned against the United States and as Afghanistan turned against the Soviet Union. One reason is that recipients increasingly resent being dependent the more aid they receive. Another – more important one – is that the aid giver becomes identified with the *government* to which the aid is being given. Even if the aid is not being used to keep a government in power, the aid giver is increasingly seen as the supporter of the incumbents; of the Colonels in Greece, for instance, or of the Shah of Iran. When the incumbents are removed, even by peaceful means, the successor government is almost forced to turn against the foreign power that worked with its predecessors, that is, against the aid giver.

Military aid has done damage both to the country that extended it and to the recipient. It forces the recipient to misdirect its vision, its resources, its energies towards military ends and to neglect everything else. Again and again it has created military dictators. And far too many of them then became international terrorists who used the military aid they receive to turn their country into a land-based pirate ship to terrorize the international community – as Saddam Hussein did in Iraq.

And only defence contractors are likely to be hurt if military aid is abandoned.

What to abandon in economic policy

If we have learned one thing it is that government cannot manage the economic 'weather'. Government cannot effectively prevent or overcome short-term economic fluctuations such as a recession.

No one before 1929 – as said earlier – expected government to be able to manage the economic weather. Since then every government in every country promises to be able to cure recessions. But this is pure quackery. No government has so far been able to deliver on this promise. Political leaders will have to learn to say 'No one knows how to manage the economy short-term any more than the physician knows how to cure the common cold. We had better keep our hands off it.'

A corollary to this is, however, that government needs to regain the ability to avert *major depressions*. Government spending to increase consumption has been proven not to be the way to do this. Wherever tried, the public hoarded the added purchasing power rather than spending it. The last time this happened in the United States was in Jimmy Carter's presidency. But it regularly happened in every earlier such attempt since the first one: Franklin D. Roosevelt's attempt to cure the Great Depression by government creation of purchasing power. The one result was the severe economic collapse of 1936/1937. The one effective way to counteract a depression, that is, a prolonged period of structural change, is through investment in the infrastructure – and after prolonged boom periods the infrastructure – roads, bridges, harbours, public buildings, public lands – is always in bad repair. For governments to be able to finance such investments requires, however, that they operate with a balanced budget during good times – and during recessions as well. They will then have the ability to raise money, especially through borrowing, when there is need to do so. In other words, governments have to learn again to keep deficits as the weapon of last resort. In peacetime deficits are to be used – if at all – only to finance permanent improvements of the economy's wealth-generating capacity.

Altogether in the economic sphere we need to abandon the theory of the *Fiscal State* on which the Megastate has been operating, especially in the English-speaking world. What is needed is a return from a *social* policy of taxation to an *economic* one. To be sure, taxation needs to be tempered by considerations of equity and justice. To be sure, there is room for taxation which penalizes, even harshly, socially undesirable activities whether this be child labour or grossly excessive executive salaries such as have become the norm in American business in the last 20 or 25 years.

But these are qualifiers. The centre of tax policy has to be a socially neutral policy.

Is any of this politically feasible? The answer is 'yes' – it is just not easy.

To abandon anything is always bitterly resisted. People in any organization, including bureaucrats and politicians, are always attached to the obsolete; the obsolescent; the things that should have worked but didn't; the things that once were productive and no longer are. They are most attached to what in an earlier book* I called 'investments in managerial ego'. But it is also always in such areas and in such ventures in which the largest number of people are employed. For every organization tends to deploy its ablest people to 'problems' rather than to results, and especially an organization in trouble.

To abandon anything is thus difficult – but only for a fairly short spell. Six months after such efforts have been abandoned everybody wonders: 'Why did it take us so long'?

The belief that the Fiscal State can effectively redistribute income and thereby reform society through taxation and subsidies has been decisively disproven. The least egalitarian countries are those that have tried hardest to redistribute income: the Soviet Union, the United States, Britain. All they accomplished was to give us the Pork-Barrel State – surely the most dangerous degenerative disease the body politic is suffering from. No one knows so far how we can get rid of this legalized looting of the commonwealth. It may require constitutional innovations – perhaps a new public agency independent of both legislature and executive, which audits spending proposals and determines whether this or that proposed outlay is actually in the public interest and compatible with public policy. (Such an audit would resemble in the public sphere the 'business audit' proposed in Chapter 3 for the governance of corporations.) The idea will be called naive, not to say Utopian. Legislatures can be expected to resist any attempt to discipline themselves. Actually a good many legislators – in the United States, in Japan, in the UK, in France and Germany – would welcome such an outside check on their undiscipline. They cannot apply it themselves – or believe they cannot do so – without being punished by the special-interest groups. But they also know that the pork-barrel process

---

* *Managing for Results* (London: Heinemann, 1964).

is undermining their own position and their standing with their constituents, apart from destroying their self-respect. In all countries money for government spending will be increasingly scarce in the years to come. This might make the control of pork-barrel spending increasingly attractive. That it is badly needed, no one doubts any more.

Abandonment comes first in the turnaround strategy. Until it has been accomplished nothing else gets done. All resources are then still allocated to the 'problems'. The acrimonious and emotional debate over what to abandon holds everybody in its grip. There are those who argue that there should be 'one more try'. There are others who seek – fruitlessly – for a 'compromise'. There are the charlatans who promise to be able to amputate a gangrenous limb without inflicting pain, and so on, and so on. Until abandonment is out of the way, no work gets done.

What to concentrate on

Rebirth can begin once the dead are buried. It starts with asking: what has been successful? Where have we had results? What should we concentrate on?

The economic performance of Japan and Germany in the last 40 years both teach the same lesson. These countries focused on the economic 'climate' instead of on the economic 'weather'. The aim of their economic policies has not been to make the patient *feel* good. It has been to make the patient healthy and to keep the patient healthy. It has been to create an economic environment in which the economy can grow, acquires resistance to infection, injury and disease; acquires ability to adapt and to change rapidly; and stays competitive.

Both countries almost immediately lost momentum, however, as soon as they attempted to 'control the weather'. The German economy began to drift in 1989 when the government – in order to buy the votes of the newly reunified East Germans – switched to massive deficit spending to jack up consumption. The attempt of the Japanese to offset short-term export contraction following the devaluation of the US dollar in the mid-1980s by pushing up domestic consumer spending almost immediately triggered a runaway speculative boom in stock market and real estate prices. All it did was to create the 'bubble economy' which then finally 'burst' in 1991 and 1992.

Creating the right climate is not the same thing as keeping taxes low. The contention of the supply-side economists that low taxes by themselves guarantee economic health and growth has not been proven. Their contention that high taxes inevitably mean economic stagnation has been decisively disproven. Japan has had very high income tax rates all along. The *incidence of taxation*, as said earlier is more important than the rate of taxation. The proper aim of fiscal policy has to be encouragement of investment in knowledge and in the human resource, in productive facilities in business, and in infrastructure. This has been the secret of all the 'economic successes' of the last half-century, of Japan, of Germany, and of the 'Four Asian Tigers': South Korea, Hong Kong, Singapore and Taiwan. All were successful as long as they stuck to policies that focus on creating the economic climate and as long as they largely ignored the economic weather.

Beyond the Nanny State

The last step in a turnaround strategy is to look at the policies and activities that have been partly successful and partly unsuccessful. One tries to determine what it is that has been unsuccessful so that one can stop doing it. The first question is: what should be abandoned? But then one asks: and what works? And what should we do more of?

This question has already been discussed in respect to one manifestation of the Megastate: the Cold-War State. Arms control has worked – in part; the Cold-War State has not. What is needed now is transnational arms control. Arms control through 'mutually assured destruction' has proven economically unbearable even for the richest nation, and powerless to halt the spread of terrorist arms and their proliferation.

There is a second sphere in which the results have been mixed: the social sphere. The Nanny State itself has had very few results. Very few results have been achieved by government's being the *doer* in the social sphere. But where we have had non-governmental action by autonomous community organizations we have achieved a great deal. The post-capitalist society and the post-capitalist polity require a new, a *Social Sector* – both to satisfy social needs and to restore meaningful citizenship and community.

This, however, is such an important – and such a novel – subject that it deserves a chapter of its own.

9

Citizenship through the social sector

Social needs will grow in two areas. They will grow in what has traditionally been considered *charity*: helping the poor, the disabled, the helpless, the victims. They will grow – perhaps even faster – in respect to services that aim at *changing* the *community* and at changing the *human being*.

In a transition period the number of people in need always grows. There are the huge masses of refugees all over the globe, victims of war and social upheaval, of racial, ethnic, political, religious persecution, of government incompetence and of government cruelty. Even in the most settled and most stable societies there will be people whom the shift to knowledge work leaves behind. It takes a generation or two before a society and its population catch up with radical changes in the composition of the workforce and in the demand for skills and knowledge. It takes some time – the best part of a generation, judging by historical experience – before the productivity of service workers will have been raised sufficiently to provide them with a 'middle-class' standard of living.

The needs will grow equally – perhaps even faster – in the *sec-*

ond areas of social services, services which do not dispense charity but attempt to make a difference in the community and to *change the human being*. Such services were practically unknown in earlier times – whereas charity has been with us for millennia. They have mushroomed in the last hundred years, especially in the United States. But these services will be needed even more in the next decades. One reason is the rapid increase in old people in all developed countries, most of whom live alone and want to live alone. Another reason is the growing sophistication of health care and medical care, calling for health-care research, health-care education and for more and more medical and hospital facilities. There is the growing need for continuing education of adults. There is the need created by the growing number of one-parent families. The community-service sector is likely to be one of the true 'growth sectors' of developed economies – whereas we can hope that the need for charity will eventually subside again.

The attempt to satisfy these needs through the Nanny State has largely failed – or at least as an attempt to have government run and manage these services. The first conclusion from the experience of the Nanny State is therefore for government to stop being a doer and manager in the social sphere and to confine itself to being the policy maker. This means that in the social sphere, as in the economic sphere, there is need to 'contract out', to 'outsource', to 'unbundle'. Just as we are restructuring the business enterprise by contracting out support work, clerical work, maintenance work, government needs to be restructured by contracting out the doing of work in the social sector.

There is an additional reason: the need to raise the productivity of service work and service worker. Government is the largest employer of service workers; yet service workers in government have the lowest productivity. As long as they are government employees their productivity cannot go up. A government agency must be a 'bureaucracy'. It must (indeed it should) subordinate productivity to rules and regulations. It must be wrapped in 'red tape'. It must focus on proper paperwork rather than on results. Otherwise it soon becomes a gang of thieves. And the largest single number of government employees in all developed countries work on delivering services; on running such services; on *doing* in the social sector. Contracting out the doing is equally necessary to get the social sector done.

None of the US programmes of the last 40 years in which we

tried to tackle a social problem through government action has produced significant results. But independent non-profit agencies have had impressive results.

Public schools in inner cities (e.g. New York, Detroit or Chicago) have been going downhill at an alarming rate. Church-run schools (especially schools of the Roman Catholic dioceses) have had startling successes – in the same communities and with children from similarly broken families and of the same racial and ethnic groups. The only successes in fighting alcoholism and drug abuse – and very substantial ones – have been achieved by such independent organizations as Alcoholics Anonymous, the Salvation Army or the Samaritans. The only successes in getting 'welfare mothers' – single mothers, often Black or Hispanic – off welfare and back into paid work and into a stable family life have been achieved by autonomous, non-profit organizations such as the Judson Center in Royal Oak, Michigan (on this, see my 1990 book *Managing the Non-Profit Organization*). Improvements in major health-care areas, e.g. in the prevention and treatment of cardiac disease and of mental illness, have largely been the work of independent non-profit organizations. The American Heart Association or the American Mental Health Association, for instance, sponsor and finance the needed research and take the lead in educating both the medical community and the public in prevention and treatment.

To foster autonomous community organizations in the social sector is therefore an important step in turning around government and in making it perform again.

The greatest contribution the autonomous community organization makes is as the new *centre of meaningful citizenship*. The Megastate has all but destroyed citizenship. To restore it, the post-capitalist polity needs a 'Third Sector' in addition to the two generally recognized ones, the 'private sector' of business and the 'public sector' of government. It needs an autonomous *Social Sector*.

Patriotism is not enough

Patriotism is the willingness to die for one's country. Earlier in this century the Marxists had prophesied that the working class would no longer be patriots. Their allegiance would be to their class rather than to their country. This turned out false prophesy. People – and especially the working class – are still willing to die for their country, even in the least popular of wars.

'Patriotism is not enough', said the English nurse Edith Cavell (1865-1915), as she was led to her execution by the Germans for having sheltered escaping British prisoners of war in the Belgian hospital which she ran. There has to be citizenship as well. Citizenship is the willingness to *contribute* to one's country. It is the willingness to *live* for one's country. To restore citizenship is a central need of the post-capitalist polity.

Patriotism, the willingness to die for one's country, has been universal. But citizenship is a distinctly Western invention. It was in effect what Athens and Rome in their glory were all about. And the finest political statement of the Western tradition is about citizenship – the rousing speech which the Greek historian Thucydides put in the mouth of Pericles, the Athenian leader.

Citizenship disappeared with the collapse of Rome. The Middle Ages did not have citizens. Feudal lords had retainers, cities had burghers, the church had communicants – but no one had citizens. Nor did Japan have citizens before the Meiji Restoration of 1867. The *Daimyo*, the Lord, had retainers, the urban centres had craft guilds, the religious sects had worshipers. But there were no citizens.

The national state re-invented citizenship and was built on it. What citizenship means in terms of rights and obligations has ever since been a central issue of political theory and political practice.

As a legal term, citizenship is a term of identification rather than of action. As a *political term* citizenship means active commitment. It means responsibility. It means making a difference in one's community, one's society, one's country.

In the Megastate political citizenship no longer functions. Even if the country is small, the affairs of government are so far away that individuals cannot make a difference. Individuals can vote – and we have learned the hard way these last decades how important a right voting is. Individuals can pay taxes – and again we have learned the hard way these last decades that this is a meaningful obligation. But the individuals cannot take responsibility, cannot take action to make a difference. Without citizenship, however, the polity is empty. There can be nationalism. Without citizenship it is likely to degenerate from patriotism into chauvinism.

Without citizenship there cannot be the responsible commitment which creates the citizen and which in the last analysis holds together the body politic. Nor can there be satisfaction and pride that come from making a difference. Without it the political unit, whether called state or empire, can be a 'power'. Power is then the only thing that holds it together. But to be able to act in a rapidly changing and dangerous world, the post-capitalist polity must re-create citizenship.

The need for community

There is equal need to restore community. Traditional communities no longer have much integrating power. They cannot survive the mobility which knowledge confers on the individual. Traditional communities, we have now learned, were held together far less by what their members had in common than by necessity, if not by coercion and fear.

There is a great deal of talk these days about the disintegration of the family. To some extent this is a misunderstanding. To be sure, a substantial number of American marriages – and of marriages in the developed world altogether – end in divorce. But marriages do not last shorter than they lasted 100 or 150 years ago. They probably last longer. A 100 or 150 years ago it was death that dissolved them rather than divorce.

The traditional family was a necessity. In nineteenth-century fiction there are, by and large, mostly what we would now call 'broken families'. But they had to stay together no matter how great their hatred, their loathing, their fear of each other. 'Family is where they have to take you in' was a nineteenth-century saying. Family before this century provided practically all the social services available. What family did not provide nobody else provided. To cling to family was a necessity. To be repudiated by family was catastrophe. A stock figure of American plays and movies, as late as the 1920s, was the cruel father who threw out the daughter when she came home with an illegitimate child. And she then had only two choices: to commit suicide or to become a prostitute.

Family is actually becoming more important to most people. But it is becoming so as a voluntary bond, as a bond of affection, of attachment, of mutual respect, rather than as a bond of necessity. Today's young people, once they have grown out of adolescent rebellion, feel a much greater need than my generation did to be close to their parents and to their siblings.

Still, family is no longer *the* community. But people do need a community. They need it particularly in the sprawling huge cities and in the suburbs in which more and more of us live. One can no longer count – as one could in the rural village – on neighbours who have the same interests, the same concerns, the same occupations, the same ignorance, and who altogether live in the same world. Even if the family bond is close, one cannot count on family. Geographic and occupational mobility mean that people no longer stay in the place, the class, the culture where they were born, where their parents live, where their siblings and their cousins live. The community that is needed in post-capitalist society – and especially needed by the knowledge worker – *has to be based on commitment and compassion* rather than being imposed by proximity and isolation.

The vanishing plant community

Forty years ago I thought that this community would come into being at the place of work. In my 1942 book *The Future of Industrial Man*, my 1949 book *The New Society* (both to be reissued soon by Transaction Publishers) and in my 1954 book *The Practice of Management*, I talked of the *plant community* as the place that would give the individual status and function, and the responsibility of self government.

This is what the Japanese have realized to a considerable extent. But, as said earlier, even in Japan the plant community is not going to work much longer, at least not for knowledge workers. It is becoming increasingly clear that the Japanese plant community is far less based on belonging than it is based on fear. A worker in a Japanese large company with its seniority-wage system who loses his job past age 30 has become virtually unemployable for the rest of his life. But that is rapidly going as Japan is moving from serious shortages of jobs – the norm as recently as 1960 – to serious shortages of available labour.

In the West the plant community never took root. I still strongly maintain that the employee has to be given the maximum of responsibility and self-control – the idea that underlay my advocacy of the plant community. The knowledge-based organization has to become a responsibility-based organization.

But individuals, and especially knowledge workers, need a meaningful sphere of social life, of personal relationships, and of contributions outside and beyond the job, outside and beyond the organization, and indeed outside and beyond their own specialized knowledge area.

The volunteer as citizen

The one area in which this need can be satisfied is the social sector. There individuals can contribute. They can have responsibility. This can make a difference. They can be 'volunteers'. This is already happening in the United States.

In most other developed countries the volunteer tradition was crushed by the Welfare State. In Japan, for instance, temples and Shinto shrines were active centres of community service with strong participation by local volunteers. The 1867 Meiji Restoration 'Westernized' by making religion into a government function – and both the volunteers and the temples' community service soon disappeared. In Britain, all through the nineteenth century, charity was a community activity and seen as a responsibility of the well-to-do. After 1890, with the growing belief in government as the master of society, most of this disappeared. The Salvation Army – founded in London in 1878 – is one of the few survivors of what was a flourishing culture of community service in Victorian times. And in France *any* community action that is not organized and controlled by government has been suspect since Napoleon, and is in fact almost considered subversive.

The denominational diversity of American churches, the strong emphasis on the local autonomy of states, counties, cities, and the community tradition of isolated frontier settlements slowed the politization and centralization of social activities in the United States. As a result, that country now has almost a million nonprofits active in the social sector. They represent as much as one-tenth of the GNP – one-quarter of that sum raised by donations from the public, another quarter paid by government for specific work (e.g. to administer health-care reimbursement programmes), the rest fees for services rendered (e.g. tuition paid by students attending private universities or money made by the 'art stores' to be found now in every American museum).

The non-profits have become America's biggest employer. Every other American adult – 90 million altogether – works at least three hours a week as 'unpaid staff', that is, as a volunteer for a non-profit organization, for churches and hospitals, for health-care agencies, for community services like the Red Cross, Boy Scouts and Girl Scouts, for rehabilitation services like the Salvation Army and Alcoholics Anonymous, for shelters for battered wives and for tutoring inner-city Black children. By the year 2000 or 2010 the number of such 'unpaid staff' people should have risen to 120 million and their average hours of work to five per week.

These volunteers are no longer 'helpers'. They have become 'partners'. Non-profit organizations in the United States increasingly have a full-time paid executive. But increasingly the rest of the management team are volunteers. They increasingly run the organization. The greatest change has taken place in the American Catholic Church. In one major diocese lay *women* now actually run all the parishes as 'Parish Administrators'. The priests say Mass, and dispense the Sacraments. Everything else, including all the social and community work of the parishes, is done by 'unpaid staff' led by the Parish Administrator.

The main reason for this upsurge of volunteer participation in the United States is not an increase in need. It is the search on the part of the volunteers for community, for commitment, for contribution. The great bulk of the new volunteers are not retired people. They are husbands and wives in the professional, two-earner family, people in their thirties and forties, well-educated, affluent, busy. They enjoy their jobs. But they feel the need to do something where 'we make a difference', to use the phrase one hears again and again – whether that means running a Bible class in the local church; teaching Black children the multiplication table; or visiting old people back home from a long stay in hospital and helping them with their rehabilitation exercises.

What the US non-profits do for their volunteers may well be more important than what they do for the recipients of their services.

The Girl Scouts are one of the few American organizations that have become racially integrated. In their troops girls regardless of colour or national origin – White, Blacks, Hispanics, Asians –

work together and play together. But the greatest contribution of the integration-drive which the Girl Scouts began in the 1970s, is that it recruited a large number of mothers – Black, Asians, Hispanics – into leadership positions as volunteers in integrated community work.

Similarly, the greatest attraction of the 'Pastoral' churches, the rapid growth of which may be the most important American social phenomenon of the closing decade of this century, is the effective community activity they offer to their volunteers. These churches are almost totally volunteer-staffed. One of the largest of them has 13,000 members but only 150 paid staff people, including the senior pastor. Yet it does more community work than any traditional church has ever done. Everyone who joins the congregation is expected, after attending for a few Sundays, to start working for a church activity – either in the church itself or in the outside community. A few months later he or she will then be asked to take over the management of such an activity. Everyone is expected to be a 'leader'.

Citizenship in and through the social sector is not a panacea for the ills of post-capitalist society and post-capitalist polity. But it may be a prerequisite for tackling these ills. It restores the civic responsibility that is the mark of citizenship, and the civic pride that is the mark of community.

The need is greatest where community and community organizations – and citizenship altogether – have been most thoroughly damaged, and, in fact, have been almost totally destroyed: in the ex-Communist countries. Government in these countries has not only been totally discredited. It has become totally impotent. It may take years before the successor-governments to the Communists – in Czechoslovakia and in Kazakhstan, in Russia, Poland, the Ukraine – can competently carry out the tasks which only government can do: manage money and taxes; run the military and the courts; conduct foreign relations. In the meantime only autonomous, local, non-profits – that is, organizations of the social sector based on volunteers and releasing the spiritual energies of people – can provide both the social services the society needs and the leadership development the polity needs.

Different societies and different countries will surely structure the social sector quite differently. The churches, for instance, are unlikely to play in Western Europe the key role they play in a still largely Christian America. Membership in the employee community may well remain in Japan the central focus of community and the badge of community membership, especially for rank-and-file workers. But every developed country needs an autonomous, self-governing social sector of community organizations. It needs it to provide the needed community services. It needs it above all to provide the bonds of community and to restore active citizenship. Historically community was fate. In the post-capitalist society and polity community has to become commitment.

Part Three

Knowledge

10

Knowledge: its economics; its productivity

At first glance, the economy seems hardly affected by the shift to knowledge as the basic resource. It seems to be 'capitalist' rather than 'post-capitalist'. But looks are deceptive.

The economy will, to be sure, remain a market economy – and a worldwide market economy. It will reach even further than did the world-market economy before World War I when there were no 'planned' economies and no 'socialist' countries. Criticism of the market as the organizer of economic activity goes back all the way to Aristotle. Most of the charges against it are well founded.* But as no less an anti-capitalist as Karl Marx pointed out more than a hundred years ago, the market for all its imperfections is still vastly superior to all other ways of organizing economic activity – something that the last 40 years have amply proven indeed. What makes the market superior is precisely that it organizes economic activity around *information*.

But while the world economy will remain a market economy and retain the market institutions, its *substance* has been radically

* Among the most cogent of such criticisms is that of Karl Polanyi (1886–1964) in his 1944 book *The Great Transformation*.

changed. If it is still 'capitalist', it is *'information capitalism'* which dominates it. The industries that have moved into the centre of the economy in the last 40 years have as their business the production and distribution of knowledge and information rather than the production and distribution of objects. The actual product of the pharmaceutical industry is knowledge; pill and prescription ointment are no more than packaging for knowledge. There are the telecommunications industries and the industries which produce information-processing tools and equipment, such as computers, semiconductors, software. There are the information producers and distributors – movies, television shows, video-cassettes. The 'non-businesses' which produce and apply knowledge, that is, education and health care, have in all developed countries grown much faster even than knowledge-based businesses.

The 'super-rich' of the old capitalism were the nineteenth-century steel barons. The 'super-rich' of the post-World War II boom are computer makers, software makers, producers of television shows, or Ross Perot, the builder of a business installing and running information systems. Such great fortunes as were made in retailing – those of Sam Walton of WalMart in the United States, Masatoshi Ito of Ito-Yokado in Japan or the Sainsbury brothers in Britain – were made by reorganizing this old business around information.

In fact whichever traditional industries managed to grow in the last 40 years did so because they restructured themselves around knowledge and information. The integrated steel mill is becoming obsolete. Even in the low-wage countries it cannot compete against the minimill. But a minimill is simply a steel maker organized around information rather than around heat.

It is no longer possible to make huge profits on doing or moving things. But it is even no longer possible to make huge profits by controlling money.

In 1910 an Austro-German Socialist, Rudolf Hilferding (1877–1941), coined the term 'Finance Capitalism'. He asserted that this was the ultimate and last stage of capitalism before the inevitable coming of socialism. In a capitalist economy, he postulated, the margin between what banks pay for money and what they charge for it widens inexorably. As a result, banks and bankers become the only profit makers and the rulers of capitalist economy. Lenin, a few years later, made this thesis the basis of his theory of Communism. This explains why Soviet planning was organized around the State Bank and controlled through the allocation of bank credit. Finance Capitalism was still socialist dogma after World War II, which explains why the post-war Labour government in Britain immediately nationalized the Bank of England and why, a few years later, the first Socialist government in France nationalized the main commercial banks.

But commercial banks are everywhere in trouble. The margin between what they pay for money and what they get for it is shrinking steadily. They cannot make a good living by earning a return on money. Increasingly they can only make a living – let alone a profit – by receiving fees for information.

Increasingly there is less and less *return* on the traditional resources, labour, land and (money) capital. The only – at least the main – producers of wealth are information and knowledge.

The economics of knowledge

How knowledge behaves as an *economic* resource we do not yet fully understand. We have not had enough experience to formulate a theory and to test it. We can only say so far that we need such a theory. We need an economic theory that puts knowledge into the centre of the wealth-producing process. Such a theory alone can explain the present economy. It alone can explain economic growth. It alone can explain innovation. It alone can explain how the Japanese economy works and, above all, why it works. It alone can explain why newcomers, especially in high-tech fields, can, almost overnight, sweep the market and drive out all competitors, no matter how well entrenched they are – as the Japanese did in consumer electronics and in the US automobile market.

So far there are no signs of an Adam Smith or a David Ricardo of knowledge. But the first studies of the economic behaviour of knowledge have begun to appear.*

* Examples are the work done by Paul Romer of the University of California, Berkeley, such as his two articles: 'Endogenous Technical Change' in the *Journal of Political Economy* (1990) and 'Are Nonconvexities Important for Understanding Growth?' in *American Economic Review* (1990); the work done by Maurice Scott of Oxford, especially his book *A New View of Economic Growth* (Oxford University Press, 1989); and the article by Jacob T. Schwartz, a New York University mathematician and computer scientist, 'America's Economic-Technological Agenda for the 1990s' in *Daedalus*, the Journal of the American Academy of Arts and

These studies make it crystal-clear that the knowledge-based economy does not behave the way existing theory assumes an economy to behave. We therefore know that the new economic theory, the theory of a knowledge-based economy, will be quite different from any existing economic theory, whether Keynesian or Neo-Keynesian, Classical or Neo-Classical.

One of the economists' basic assumptions is that 'perfect competition' is the model for the allocation of resources and also for the distribution of economic rewards. Imperfect competition is common in the 'real world'. But it is assumed to be the result of outside interference with the economy, i.e. of monopoly; of patent protection; of government regulation, and so on. But in the knowledge economy imperfect competition seems to be inherent in the economy itself. Initial advantages gained through early application and exploitation of knowledge (that is, through what has come to be known as the 'learning curve') become permanent and irreversible. What this implies is that neither free-trade economics nor protectionism will by themselves work as economic policies. The knowledge economy seems to require both in balance.*

Another one of the economist's basic assumptions is that an economy is determined either by consumption or by investment. Keynesians and Neo-Keynesians (such as Milton Friedman) make it dependent on consumption; Classicists and Neo-Classicists (such as the 'Austrians') on investment. In the knowledge economy neither seems to control. There is no shred of evidence that increased *consumption* in the economy leads to greater production of knowledge. But there is also no shred of evidence that greater *investment* in the economy leads to greater production of knowledge. At least the lead times between increased consumption and knowledge production, or between increased investment and knowledge production, seem to be so long as to defy analysis – and surely too long to base either economic theory or economic policy on the correlation, whatever it might be.

Equally incompatible with traditional economic theory is the absence of a common denominator for different kinds of knowledge. Different pieces of land yield different yields; but their price

Sciences, Winter 1992 – the last a rigorous, yet jargon-free, presentation of the *economics of knowledge-based innovation*.

* This point is being made with considerable force in an (unsigned) article in *The Economist*, (4 January, 1992).

is determined by these differences, that is, by *quantity* of output. When it comes to new knowledge, there are three kinds (as already discussed in Chapter 4). There is first, continuing *improvement* of process, product, service – the Japanese, who do it best, call it *kaizen*. There is exploitation; the continuous exploitation of existing knowledge to develop new and different products, processes and services. Finally, there is genuine *innovation*. These three ways of applying knowledge to produce change in the economy (and in society as well) need to be worked at together and at the same time. They are equally needed. But their economic characteristics – their costs as well as their economic impacts – are *qualitatively* different. Altogether it is not possible – at least not so far – to *quantify* knowledge. We can, of course, estimate how much it *costs* to produce and distribute knowledge. But how much is produced – indeed what we might even mean by 'return on knowledge' – we cannot say. Yet there is no economic theory unless there is a model that expresses economic events in *quantitative* relationships. Without it there is no way to make a rational choice – and rational choices are what economics is all about.

Above all, the *amount of knowledge*, that is its quantitative aspect, is not nearly as important as the *productivity* of knowledge, that is, its qualitative impact. And this applies to old knowledge and its application as well as to new knowledge.

The productivity of knowledge

Knowledge does not come cheap. All developed countries spend something like a fifth of their GNP on the production and dissemination of knowledge. Formal schooling – schooling of young people before they enter the workforce – takes about one-tenth of GNP (up from 2% or so at the time of World War I). Employing organizations spend another 5% of GNP on the continuing education of their employees; it may be more. And 3 to 5% of GNP are spent on research and development, that is, on the production of new knowledge.

Very few countries set aside a similar portion of their GNP to form traditional (that is, money) capital. Even in Japan and Germany, the two major countries with the highest rates of capital formation, the rate exceeded one-fifth of GNP only during the years of the most feverish rebuilding and expansion in the 40 years of the post-World War II period. In the United States capital formation has not reached 20% of GNP for many years. Knowledge-formation is thus already the largest investment in every developed country. Surely, the return which a country or a company gets on knowledge must increasingly be a determining factor in their competitiveness. Increasingly, *productivity of knowledge* will be decisive in their economic and social success, and in their economic performance altogether. And we know that there are tremendous differences in the productivity of knowledge – between countries, between industries, between individual organizations. Here are some examples.

According to its production of scientific and technical knowledge, Britain should have been the world's economic leader in the post-World War II era. Antibiotics, the jet engine, the body scanner, even the computer, were British developments. But Britain did not succeed in turning these knowledge-achievements into successful products and services, into jobs, into exports, into market standing. The non-productivity of its knowledge, more than anything else, is at the root of the slow and steady erosion of the British economy.

Similar danger signs abound today in respect to the productivity of knowledge in American society. In industry after industry – from microchips to fax machines and from machine tools to copiers – American companies have generated the new technologies only to see Japanese companies develop the products and take over the markets. In the United States the additional output for each additional input of knowledge is clearly lower than that of America's Japanese competitors. In important areas the productivity of knowledge in the United States is falling behind.

Germany furnishes a different example. Post-World War II Germany – at least until 1990 and reunification – recorded an impressive economic achievement. In most industries – but also in such areas as banking and insurance – West Germany attained stronger leadership positions than were held by either Imperial Germany or pre-Hitler Germany. West Germany, year after year, exported for instance, four times as much per capita as the United States and three times as much as Japan. West Germany thus had exceedingly high productivity in old knowledge, in applying it, improving it, exploiting it. But it had extremely low productivity in new knowledge and especially in the new 'high-tech' areas: computers, telecommunications, pharmaceuticals, advanced materials, biogenetics and so on. Proportionately, West Germany invested as much money and talent in these areas as did the United States – maybe more. It produced a fair amount of new knowledge. But it has signally failed in converting the new knowledge into successful innovation. The new knowledge has remained information rather than become productive.

The most instructive example is Japan. Japan has done particularly well these last 40 years both in old manufacturing and in new knowledge-based industries. Yet Japan's meteoric rise was not based on *producing* knowledge. In technology and in management most of Japan's knowledge was produced elsewhere, most of it in the United States. Serious work in Japan on building a knowledge base at home hardly even began until the late 1970s; and even now, in the 1990s, when Japan has long become the world's second economic power, the country still imports more knowledge than it exports. At that the Japanese did not actually import a very great deal of technological (as distinct from management) knowledge. But they made superbly productive whatever knowledge they acquired.

It is likely that the *productivity of resources* will altogether become a central concern of economics in post-capitalist society. It underlies the relationship between environment and economic growth. We also face with respect to money capital a productivity problem that is quite similar to what we face with respect to the productivity of knowledge capital.

Productivity of money capital was ignored by economists until World War II. Practically all of them, including Marx, thought in terms of the quantity of capital rather than in terms of its productivity. Even Keynes distinguished only money invested and money hoarded. He took for granted the productivity of money once it had been invested.

But in the post-World War II years we began to ask: how much added production does an additional unit of invested money generate? What is the productivity of capital? It then became apparent that there are differences in the productivity of money capital and that the differences matter, and matter greatly.

At the time at which concern with productivity of capital first arose – in the late 1950s and early 1960s – central planning was all the rage, worldwide. People only asked whether the detailed top-down planning by command of the Soviet Five-Year Plans or the consensus planning of the French *Plan Indicatif* was the better way to run the economy. But almost everybody accepted that the results which planning yielded were vastly superior to the unplanned capital allocation of the market, both in total output and in output per unit of investment.

The very first attempts to measure actual performance showed conclusively that under both types of planning the productivity of capital is very low and is declining steadily. They showed that under central planning additional units of capital investment yield less and less additional output.

The French immediately acted. They shelved the *Plan Indicatif*, and with it economic planning altogether. If France had not thus changed course by 180 degrees in the early 1960s, it would today look very much the way East Germany does.

Soviet planners kept on planning. And the productivity of capital in the Soviet Empire kept on falling – to the point where it actually became negative. In the Brezhnev years agricultural investment rose steadily until it took the lion's share of all available non-defence money. But the more money the Russians poured into farming, the smaller their harvests became. And the same negative productivity of capital also engulfed civilian industries in Russia – we have no information on what happened in the defence sector. The failure of the productivity of capital more than anything else brought about the collapse of the Soviet economy in the end.

Centralization, we now know, impedes the productivity of money capital. The tremendous investments in the Third World made by the World Bank were not centrally planned. But they were – and are – highly centralized. Their productivity has been low. They have built highly visible monuments such as enormous steel mills. But they have had very little 'multiplier' effects on the whole. They have created few jobs outside the plant gates. They have rarely become economically self-sustaining, let alone profitable. Thus they act as a drag on the national economy rather than supplying it with additional investment capital.

It is highly likely that centralized planning and centralization altogether would make knowledge capital as unproductive as they make money capital unproductive.

Japanese planning for 'high-tech' knowledge is as much the rage these days as Russian and French planning for economic development was about 30 years ago. The results so far are, however, singularly unimpressive. The Japanese triumphs in high-tech industries owe very little to the much-touted government plans. Most of them have been failures, e.g. the ambitious plan to develop the 'Fifth-Generation' supercomputer. And the various US plans to beat the Japanese through government-sponsored 'consortia', that is, through centralization of innovation, have also been quite unsuccessful.

Innovation, that is, the application of knowledge to produce new knowledge, is not, as so much American folklore asserts, 'inspiration' and best done by lone individuals in their garages. It requires systematic, effort, and a high degree of organization.* But it also requires both decentralization and diversity, that is, the opposite of central planning and centralization.

The management requirements

Terms like centralization, decentralization and diversity are not terms of economics. They are *management* terms. We do not have an economic theory of the productivity of knowledge investment – we may never have one. But we have management precepts. We know, above all, that making knowledge productive is a *management responsibility*. It cannot be discharged by government. But it also cannot be done by market forces. It requires systematic, organized application of knowledge to knowledge.

The first rule may well be that knowledge has to aim high to produce results. The steps may be small and incremental. The goal has to be ambitious. Knowledge is productive only if it is applied to make a difference.

The Hungarian-American Nobel Prize winner Albert von Szent Györgyi (1893–1990) revolutionized physiology. When asked to explain his achievements he gave the credit to his teacher, an otherwise obscure professor at a provincial Hungarian university. 'When I got my doctorate,' Szent Györgyi said, 'I proposed to study flatulence – nothing was known about it and nothing is known about it still.' 'Very interesting,' the professor said. 'But no one has ever died of flatulence. If you have results – and it's a big "if" – you'd better have them where they'll make a difference.'

---

* On this see my 1985 book *Innovation and Entrepreneurship* (London: Heinemann).

'And so', Szent Györgyi said, 'I took on the study of basic chemistry and discovered the enzymes.'

Every single one of Szent Györgyi's research projects was a small step. But from the beginning he aimed high: discovering the basic chemistry of the human body. Similarly, in Japanese *kaizen*, every single step is a small one – a minor change here, a minor improvement there. But the aim is to produce by means of step-by-step improvements a few years later a radically different product, process or service. The aim is to make a difference.

To make knowledge productive further requires that it be clearly focused. It has to be highly concentrated. Whether done by an individual or by a team, the knowledge effort requires purpose and organization. It is not 'flash of genius'. It is work.

To make knowledge productive also requires the systematic exploitation of opportunities for change – what, in an earlier book* I called the 'Seven Windows of Innovation'. These opportunities have to be matched with the competences and strengths of the knowledge worker and the knowledge team.

To make knowledge productive finally requires managing time. High knowledge productivity – whether in improvement, in exploitation or in innovation – comes at the end of a long gestation period. Yet productivity of knowledge also requires a constant stream of short-term results. It thus requires the most difficult of all management achievements: balancing the long term with the short term.

Our experience in making knowledge productive has so far been gained mainly in economy and technology. But the same rules pertain to making knowledge productive in social problems, in the polity, and in respect to knowledge itself. So far, little work has been done to apply knowledge to these areas. But we need productivity of knowledge even more in these areas than we need it in the economy, in technology or in medicine.

Only connect

The productivity of knowledge requires increasing the yield from what is known – by the individual or by the group.

There is an old American story of the farmer who turns down a

---

* *Innovation and Entrepreneurship* (London: Heinemann, 1985).

proposal for a more productive farming method by saying 'I already know how to farm twice as well as I do'.

Most of us (perhaps all of us) know many times more than we put to use. The main reason is that we do not mobilize the multiple knowledges we possess. We do not use knowledges as part of one toolbox. Instead of asking 'What do I know, what have I learned, that might apply to this task?' we tend to classify tasks in terms of specialized knowledge areas.

Again and again in working with executives I find that a given challenge – in organization structure, for instance, or in technology – yields to knowledge the executive already posseses – he or she may have acquired it, for instance, in an economics course at university. 'Of course, I know that' is the standard response, 'but it's economics and not management.' This is, of course, a purely arbitrary distinction – necessary perhaps to learn and to teach a 'subject' but irrelevant as a definition of what knowledge is and what it can do. The way we traditionally organize businesses, government agencies and universities further encourages the tendency to believe that the purpose of the tools is to adorn the toolbox rather than to do work.

In learning and teaching we do have to focus on the tool. In usage we have to focus on the end result, on the task, on the work. 'Only connect' was the constant admonition of a great English novelist, E. M. Forster (1879–1970). It has always been the hallmark of the great artist but equally of the great scientist, of a Darwin, a Bohr, an Einstein. At their level the capacity to connect may be inborn and part of that mystery we call 'genius'. But, to a large extent, to connect and thus to raise the yield of existing knowledge – whether for an individual, for a team or for the entire organization – is learnable. Eventually it should become teachable. It requires a methodology for *problem definition* – more perhaps even than it requires the (now fashionable) methodology for 'problem solving'. It requires systematic analysis of the kind of knowledge and information a given problem requires, and a methodology for organizing the stages in which a given problem can be tackled – the methodology which underlies what we now call 'systems research'. It requires what might be called, 'Organizing Ignorance'* – there is always so much more ignorance around than there is knowledge.

* Which was to be the title of a book I began to write 40 years ago but never finished.

Specialization into knowledges has given us enormous performance potential in each area. But because knowledges are specialized we need also a methodology, a discipline, a process to turn potential into performance. Otherwise most of the available knowledge will not become productive. It will remain information.

Not to see the forest for the trees is a serious failing. But it is an equally serious failing not to see the trees for the forest. One can only plant individual trees, can only cut individual trees. Yet the forest is the 'ecology', the environment without which individual trees would never grow. To make knowledge productive we will have to learn to see both forest and trees. We will have to learn to connect.

The productivity of knowledge is increasingly going to be the determining factor in the competitive position of a country, an industry, a company. In respect to knowledge, no country, no industry, no company has any 'natural' advantage or disadvantage. The only advantage it can possess is in respect to how much it obtains from universally available knowledge. The only thing that increasingly will matter in national as well as in international economics is management's performance in making knowledge productive.

11

The accountable school

A technological revolution: desktop computers; satellite transmission directly into the classroom, is engulfing the school. It will transform the way we learn and the way we teach within a few decades. It will change the economics of education. From being almost totally labour-intensive schools will become highly capital-intensive.

But more drastic even – though rarely discussed as yet – will be the changes in the social position and role of the school. Though long a central institution, it has been *of* society rather than *in* society. It concerned itself with the young who were not yet citizens, not yet responsible, not yet in the workforce. In the knowledge society the school becomes the institution of the adults as well, and especially of highly schooled adults. Above all, in the knowledge society the school becomes accountable for performance and results.

In the West the school underwent an earlier technological revolution several hundred years ago. It was brought about by the printed book. This earlier technological revolution holds important lessons for today – and lessons that are not technological.

One lesson: embracing the new technology of learning and teaching is a prerequisite for national and cultural success – and equally for economic competitiveness.

The West moved into leadership throughout the world between 1500 and 1650 in large measure because it reorganized its schools around the new technology of the printed book. Conversely their refusal to redesign their schools around the printed book was a major factor in the decline of China and of Islam and in their eventually succumbing to the West. Both used printing – the Chinese had done so for centuries, of course (albeit not with movable type) – but both kept the printed book out of their schools; both rejected the printed book as a learning and teaching tool. The Islamic clergy stuck to rote learning and recitation; it saw in the printed book a threat to its authority precisely because it enables students to read on their own. In China the Confucian scholars equally rejected the printed book; they stuck to calligraphy. The printed book was incompatible with a key tenet of Chinese culture: mastery of calligraphy qualifies for rulership.

Before 1550 China and the Ottoman Empire – the political embodiment of Islam – were the world's 'superpowers', politically, militarily, economically, scientifically, culturally. Until 1550 both were in the ascendant. From 1550 on, both became increasingly stagnant. Both became inward-looking. Both increasingly went on the defensive. In the West the school came to be seen as the 'progressive' institution and as the engine of advance in all areas – in culture, in the arts, in literature, in science, in the economy, in politics and in the military. In Islam and in China the school came increasingly to be seen as a major obstacle to progress; rebellion against the school was the starting point for all reform movements in these two great civilizations.

The earlier revolution in learning demonstrates another and equally important lesson: technology itself matters less than the changes which it triggers in substance, content and focus of schooling and school. These changes in substance, content, focus are what really matters. They are effective even if there is only a minimum of change in the technology of learning and teaching.

The Japanese followed neither the Western model in their 'new' and 'modern' schools – the schools which the *bunjin* (i.e. literati, or humanist) movement of the 'Kyoto Renaissance' developed in the late eighteenth and early nineteenth centuries. Unlike the West, they did not put the printed book in the centre; in fact,

Japanese calligraphy reached its peak in the schools the *bunjin* founded in Kyoto and then spread throughout the entire country. Their schools stressed the discipline calligraphy imparts and the aesthetic perception it trains – as does Japanese education to this day. The schools of the *bunjin* did not, however, shun the printed book as the Chinese had done. They used it, and effectively. Above all, they rejected the Chinese idea of the 'scholar' as an elite group, separate from and different from ordinary folk. The *bunjin* aimed at universal literacy; wherever they went they induced the local lord to start schools for the children in his domain, open to all. And in content and substance the *bunjin* school drew heavily on everything it could learn from the West and the Western school – mostly through the Dutch traders who resided in Nagasaki. In fact, these schools of the Kyoto Renaissance of 200 years ago are perhaps the best example of that unique Japanese faculty to absorb foreign culture – in this case, both Chinese and Western culture – and to 'Japanize' it. It was the *bunjin* school which, a century later, enabled the Japanese, alone among non-Western peoples, to become a modern nation, to become 'Westernized' in economy, technology, political institutions and the military, and yet to remain profoundly 'Japanese'. Every one who transformed in the late nineteenth century the isolated and still feudal Japan of the Tokugawa Shogunate into the 'modern' Japan of the 'Meiji Restoration' had been a student in one of the *bunjin* schools and was taught by one of the great *bunjin* masters or by one of their disciples.

Technology, however important and however visible, will thus not be the most important feature of the transformation in schooling and school. Most important will be rethinking the role and function of schooling and school; their content; their focus; their purpose; their values. The technology will be very important; but primarily because it should force us to do new things rather than because it will enable us to do old things better.

Again, the earlier European revolution in learning and teaching furnishes the example. The greatest figure of this development, the one man who can be called the 'Father of the Modern School', was John Amos Comenius (1592–1670), a Czech Protestant (his original name was Komensky), driven out of his homeland by the Catholic counter-reformation that followed the defeat of the Czech uprising in 1618 against the Catholic Hapsburgs. We owe to Comenius the technology that made the printed book the effective carrier of learning and teaching; he invented the Primer and the Text Book. But these were to him only tools. His school centred in a new curriculum. It is still, by and large, what schools throughout the world consider 'education'. His aim was universal literacy. And his motivation was religious: to enable his Czech compatriots to remain Protestants and to read and study the Bible on their own, even though their religion had been suppressed and their pastors driven out by the victorious Papists.

The real challenge ahead is not technology. It is what to use it for. So far, no country has the educational system which the knowledge society needs. No country has so far tackled the major demands. No one, so far, knows 'the answers'; no one can do what is needed. But we can at least ask the questions. We can define, albeit only in rough outline, the specifications for schooling and for the schools which might answer to the realities of the post-capitalist society, the knowledge society. These specifications call for a school as different from the one that exists now as the 'modern' school for which Comenius drew up the specifications 350 years ago differed from the school that existed before the printed book. And here are the specifications:

- The school we need has to provide universal literacy of a high order – well beyond what 'literacy' means today.
- It has to imbue students on all levels and of all ages with motivation to learn and with the discipline of continuing learning.
- It has to be open to both, already highly educated people and to people who, for whatever reason, did not gain access to advanced education in their early years.
- We need schooling which imparts knowledge both as substance and as process – what the Germans differentiate as *Wissen* and *Können*.
- Finally, schooling can no longer be a monopoly of the schools. Education in the post-capitalist society has to permeate the entire society, with employing organizations of all kinds: businesses, government agencies, non-profits, becoming learning and teaching institutions, and with schools increasingly working in partnership with employers and employing organizations.

The new performance demands

Universal literacy of a very high order is the first priority. It is the foundation. Without it no society can hope to be capable of high performance in the post-capitalist world and in its knowledge society. To equip individual students with the tools to perform, to contribute and to be employable is also the first social duty of any educational system.

It is in respect to universal literacy that the new technology of learning will have its first impact. Most schools, throughout the ages, have spent endless hours on trying to teach things that are best learned rather than taught, that is, things that are being learned behaviourally and through drill, repetition, feedback. Here belong most of the subjects taught in elementary school but also a good many of the subjects taught in later stages of the educational process. Such subjects, whether reading and writing, arithmetic, spelling, historical facts, biology – and even such advanced subjects as neurosurgery, medical diagnosis and most of engineering – are best *learned* through a computer program. The teacher motivates, directs and encourages. The teacher becomes a leader and a resource.

In the school of tomorrow the students will be their own instructors, with a computer program as their own tool. In fact, the younger the students are, the more does the computer appeal to them, the more does it guide and instruct them. Historically, the elementary school has been totally labour-intensive. Tomorrow's elementary school will be heavily capital-intensive.

Yet, despite the available technology, universal literacy poses tremendous challenges. The traditional concepts of literacy no longer suffice. Reading, writing, arithmetic will be needed as they are today. But literacy now needs to go well beyond these foundations. It requires numeracy. It requires a basic understanding of science and of the dynamics of technology. It requires acquaintance with foreign languages. It also requires learning how to be effective as a member of an organization, that is, as an employee.

Universal literacy implies a clear commitment to the priority of schooling. It demands that the school, especially the school of the beginners, the children, subordinate everything to the acquisition of foundation skills. Unless the school successfully imparts these skills to the young learner it has failed in its crucial duties: to give beginners self-confidence, to give them competence, and to make them capable, a few years hence, to perform and to achieve in the post-capitalist society, the knowledge society.

This requires a reversal of the prevailing trend in modern education and especially in American education. Having, as it thought, achieved universal literacy by the end of World War I or, at the latest, by the end of World War II, American education reversed its priorities. Social reform rather than learning became the school's first priority. In the 1950s and 1960s, when we in the United States made this decision, it was probably an inevitable one. The severity and extent of the racial problem we faced forced us to make the school the agent of racial integration – and the Blacks and the legacy of the sin of slavery have been the central American challenges for 150 years and are likely to remain the central American challenges for at least another 50 or 100 years. But the schools could not do this social job. Like every other organization, the schools are good at only their own special-purpose task. Subordinating learning to social goals may have actually impeded racial integration and the advancement of Black people – as more and more of the achieving Blacks now assert. But putting social ends ahead of the goal of learning became a major factor in the decline of American basic education, that is, in the crisis of traditional literacy in the United States. Upper- and middle-class children still acquire it. The ones who need it the most do not: the children of the poor and the children of immigrants.

What is needed now is reassertion of the original purpose of the school. It is not social reform or social amelioration. It has to be individual learning. The most hopeful developments in US education may well be that this is increasingly being asserted by achieving Blacks themselves, such as the Black woman legislator who in Milwaukee, Wisconsin, pushed through a 'voucher plan' against the strident opposition of the educational establishment. This plan enables parents to choose for their child a school which focuses on learning and demands learning.

This will be attacked by Liberals and Progressives as an elitist – and indeed a racist – position. But the most elitist school, the Japanese school, has created the most egalitarian society. Even those who do not shine in the intensely competitive educational race still acquire what by any traditional standard is extremely high literacy and an extremely high ability to achieve and to perform in modern society. Yet in the Japanese school literacy is put first and everything else is subordinated to it. But there are also enough American schools around by now in which the most disadvantaged Black children learn because it is expected of them and demanded of them.

Learning to learn

'Literacy' traditionally meant subject knowledge, e.g. the ability to do multiplication or a little knowledge of American history. But the knowledge society equally needs *process knowledge* – something the schools have rarely even tried to teach.

In the knowledge society people have to learn how to learn. Indeed, in the knowledge society subjects may matter less than the students' capacity to continue learning and their motivation to do so. Post-capitalist society requires life-long learning. For this we need a discipline of learning. But life-long learning also requires that learning be alluring, indeed, that it become a high satisfaction in itself if not something the individual craves.

Of all educational systems today, only the Japanese try to equip their students with a discipline for learning. The Japanese student who tests so high on a maths test at 18, 10 years later remembers no more maths than the American 28-year-old who tested so abysmally low 10 years earlier. But the Japanese come out of school having learned how to study, how to persist, how to learn.

But the Japanese discipline of learning – the discipline of the 'examination hell' of the university entrance exam – does not motivate. Based on fear and pressure, it quenches the desire to keep on learning. And it is this desire we need.

In America's liberal-arts colleges, by contrast, learning is enjoyable for many students. But it is enjoyment alone. It is bereft of discipline. It mistakes 'feeling good' for achievement, and 'being stimulated' for discipline.

Actually we do know what to do. In fact, for hundreds, if not for thousands, of years we have been creating both the motivation for continuing learning, and the needed discipline. The good teachers of artists do it; the good coaches of athletes do it; so do the good 'mentors' in an organization of whom we hear so much these days in the literature of management development. They lead their students to achievement that is so great that it surprises the achiever and creates excitement and motivation – especially the motivation for the rigorous, disciplined, persistent work and practice which continuous learning requires.

There are few things more boring than practising scales. Yet the greater and the more accomplished pianists are, the more faithfully do they practise their scales, hour after hour, day after day, week after week. Similarly, the better surgeons are, the more faithfully do they practise tying sutures, hour after hour, day after day, week after week. Pianists do their scales for months on end for an infinitesimally small improvement in technical ability. But this then enables them to *achieve* the musical result they already hear in their inner ear. Surgeons tie sutures for months on end for an infinitesimally small improvement in their finger dexterity. But this then enables them to speed up an operation and thus save a life. *Achievement is addictive.*

But such achievement is not doing a little less poorly what one is not particularly good at. The achievement that motivates is doing exceptionally well what one is already good at. Achievement has to be based on the student's strengths – as has been known for millennia by every teacher of artists, every coach of athletes, every mentor. In fact, finding the student's strengths and focusing them on achievement is the best definition of *teacher* and *teaching*. It is the definition in the *Dialogue on the Teacher* by one of the greatest teachers of the Western tradition, St Augustine of Hippo (354–420).

Schools and schoolteachers know this too, of course. But they have rarely been allowed to focus on the strengths of students and to challenge them. Instead they have perforce had to focus on weaknesses. Practically all the time in the classroom – at least until graduate school at the university – is spent on remedying weaknesses. It is spent on producing respectable mediocrity.

Students do need to acquire minimal competence in core skills. They do need remedial work. They do need to acquire mediocrity. But in the traditional school there is practically no time for anything else. The proudest products of the traditional school, 'the all-round A students', are the ones who satisfy mediocre standards across the board. They are not the ones who achieve; they are the ones who comply. But, to repeat, the traditional school had no choice. To give every student adequacy in the foundation skills is the first task. It could only be accomplished – even in a small class – by focusing on the weaknesses of students and on remedying them.

Here the new technologies might make the greatest difference. They free teachers from spending most, if not all, their time on routine learning, on remedial learning, on repetitive learning. Teachers will still need to lead in these activities. But most of their time has traditionally been spent on 'follow-up'. Teachers, in an old phrase, spend most of their time not being teachers but being 'teaching assistants'. And that the computer does well, does indeed better than a human being. Teachers, we can hope, will thus increasingly have the time to identify the strengths of individuals, to focus on them and to lead students to achievement. They will, we can expect, have the time to *teach*.

But even if technology enables them to do it, will the school change its attitude and focus on strengths? Will it be willing to teach 'individuals' rather than 'students'? School and teacher will still have to say: 'Betsy (or John), you need to do more practise on long division; here are the examples for you to work through.' School and teacher will still have to check that Betsy or John then actually does the work. They will still have to sit down with Betsy or John to explain, to demonstrate, to encourage. But with the computer as the teaching assistant, teachers will not have to sit down with Betsy or John to supervise the actual work – which is where they now spend all, or at least most, of their time. But will they then be willing to say: 'Betsy, you draw so well; why don't you draw the portraits of all the kids in the class?'

There is a second process-knowledge to be taught by the schools – or at least to be learned in them: the process needed to obtain what in the previous chapter I called the 'yield' from knowledge. As said earlier, the place to accomplish this will probably be in practice rather than in school. The only educational institutions which are so far concerned with the yield from knowledge are 'professional' schools, e.g. engineering schools, schools of medicine, law schools, management schools. For these are the schools which focus on practice rather than on theory. But everyone will have to be able to raise the yield from knowledge. This requires that the process – the concepts; the diagnosis; the skills – will have to be made teachable, or at least learnable. This is surely an educational challenge, and, as such, a challenge for the schools.

The school in society

The school has been a central social institution for a long time – in the West at least since the Renaissance, even longer in the Orient. But it has been 'of society' rather than 'in society'. It has been a separate institution. It rarely, if ever, combined with any other institution; in the West it did so only in the very early days, in the Benedictine monasteries of the early Middle Ages, whose schools primarily trained future monks rather than the laity. And the school was not for grown people; the root of the word 'pedagogy' – *paidos* – is the Greek word for boy.

That the school will now increasingly be *in* society may therefore be as radical a change as any change in teaching and learning methods, in subject matter, and in teaching and learning process. School will continue to teach the young. But with learning becoming a life-long activity rather than something one stops when becoming a 'grown-up', schools will have to be organized for life-long learning. Schools will have to become 'open systems'.

Schools – almost everywhere – are organized on the assumption that a student has to enter every stage at a given age and with a prescribed and standardized preparation. In the United States one starts kindergarten at age 5, elementary school at age 6, middle school at age 12, high school at age 15, college or university at age 18, and so on. If one misses one of these steps (except kindergarten) one is forever out of step and rarely permitted back in.

For the traditional school this is a self-evident axiom, and almost a law of nature. But it is incompatible with the nature of knowledge and with the demands of the knowledge society, the post-capitalist society. What is needed now is a new axiom: 'The more schooling a person has, the more often he or she will need more schooling.'

In the United States, doctors, lawyers, engineers, business executives are increasingly expected to go back to school every few years lest they become obsolete. Outside of the United States, however, the return of adults to formal schooling is still the exception – and particularly the return of adults to advanced schooling in the very fields in which they have already acquired substantial knowledge and an advanced degree. In Japan it is still almost unknown – but so it is in France, in Italy and, by and large, in Germany, England and Scandinavia. It will have to become standard in all developed countries.

Even more novel is the need to make the educational system open-ended, that is, to allow people to enter its stages at any age.

In the United States this is happening quite fast. And there is England's Open University. But these are only beginnings so far.

The knowledge society can ill afford to waste knowledge potential. And the degree has also become the passport to knowledge jobs. Even in countries like the United States and Japan, in which very large numbers of young people go on to university, many more stop their schooling by the time they are 16 or 18. There is no reason to believe that most of these people lack the intellectual endowment for knowledge work. All our experience proves the opposite. What distinguishes them from the young people who go on to university is often only the lack of money. A fair number of very bright young people do not go on to university because they are mature at age 18 and want to be adults rather than continue in the cocoon of adolescence. Ten years later many want to go back. Then – as everyone who has taught them will testify – they become challenging students if only because of their superior motivation. They now *want* to take on advanced work; the 19-year-olds do so because they are *told* to do it.

But even more important: keeping open access to advanced education, regardless of age or prior educational credentials, is a *social necessity*. The *individual* service worker *must* have the opportunity to move into knowledge work. This, in effect, means that the post-capitalist society has to create an educational system which, to use a computer term, offers 'random access'. Individuals must be able at any stage in their life to continue their formal education and to qualify for knowledge work. Society needs to be willing to accept people into whatever work they are qualified for, regardless of their age.

No society today is organized for this. In fact, most developed countries are organized to keep people in the station in which they began their working careers. The system is most rigid in Japan, but nearly as rigid in Europe as well. The United States has gone furthest in creating educational opportunities for adults. The growth area in American education these last 20 years has been continuing education of adults at any age – in respect to the foundations, that is, in respect to high-school and college degrees, and in offering additional and more advanced knowledge in their specialties to already highly educated people. This gives the United States a tremendous advantage over other developed countries. But even in the United States there is still reluctance to accept people in knowledge work unless they have acquired the basic qualifications fairly early in life.

Schools as partners

Schooling will no longer be what schools do. It will increasingly be a joint venture in which schools are partners rather than monopolists. In many areas the schools will also be only one of the available teaching and learning institutions in competition with other purveyors of teaching and learning.

School, as has been said before, has traditionally been where you learn; job has been where you work. The line will become increasingly blurred. School will increasingly be the place where adults continue learning even though they are working full-time. They will come back to school for a three-day seminar; for a weekend course; for an intensive three weeks' stint; or to take courses on two evenings each week for several years until they acquire a degree. But the job will equally be a place where adults continue learning. Training is, of course, nothing new. But it used to be restricted to the beginner.

Increasingly, training in one form or another will also become life-long. The adult, and especially the adult with advanced knowledge, will increasingly be as much trainer as trainee, as much teacher as student.

In the United States, employers – businesses, governments, the military – already spend almost as much money on training adult employees as the country spends on educating the young in its formal schools.

What is yet to come is partnership between schools and employing institutions. The Germans in their apprenticeship programmes have had schools and employers working together for more than 150 years training the young. But increasingly schools and employing institutions will have to learn to work together in the advanced education of adults as well. This task – whether advanced education of already highly educated people or make-up education for people who, for one reason or another, failed to gain access to higher education in the early years – will be increasingly carried out in all kinds of partnerships, alliances, internships in which schools and other organizations work together. The schools need the stimulus from working with adults and the employing organizations fully as much as the adults and their employing organizations need the stimulus of working with schools.

The accountable school

We talk of 'good schools' and of 'poor schools', of 'prestige schools' and of 'also rans'. In Japan a few universities – Tokyo, Kyoto, Keio, Waseda, Hitotsubashi – largely control access to career opportunities in major companies and government agencies. In France the *Grandes Ecoles* enjoy a similar position of power and prestige. And while no longer Academia's absolute monarchs, Oxford and Cambridge are still the 'superpowers' of English higher education. We also go in for all kinds of measurements: the proportion of graduates of a particular liberal-arts college who go on to acquire a doctorate; the number of books in the college's library; the number of graduates of an American suburban high school who get accepted by the college of their first choice; the popularity of different universities among students. But we have barely begun to ask: what are *results* in this school? What should they be?

These questions would have come up anyhow. In this century education has become *much too expensive* not to be held accountable. As said already in the preceding chapters, in developed countries expenditures on the school system have skyrocketed from 2% of the GNP of developed countries around 1913 to 10% 80 years later. But schools are also becoming *much too important* not to be held accountable – for thinking through what their results should be as well as for their performance in attaining these results. To be sure, different school systems and different schools will and should give different answers to these questions. But every school system and every school will soon be required to ask them, and to take them seriously. We shall no longer accept the schoolmaster's age-old excuse for malperformance: 'The students are lazy and stupid.' With knowledge the central resource of society, lazy students or poor students are the responsibility of the school. There are only schools that perform and schools that do not perform.

The schools are already losing their monopoly as providers of schooling. There has always been competition between different schools – in France with its intense rivalry between government schools and Catholic schools or in the United States between different colleges and universities. In few industries is competition as keen – or as ruthless – as it is between 'prestige schools' in developed countries. But increasingly the competition will be between schools and 'non-schools', with different kinds of institutions entering the field, each offering a different approach to schooling.

One example of what can be expected is the large American company which is starting to compete with major business schools. It is marketing to other companies the executive-management programme which it developed for its own managers, and is about to offer this programme also to government agencies and to the armed services. Another example are the Japanese *juku*, the 'cram schools' which now enroll a very large proportion of Japanese middle- and high-school students. And there is also the American publisher who recently launched a company to build 600 schools within the next 5 years. They are planned to charge moderate fees – no more than the average cost of a child in the public school – yet they are to be highly profitable. And they intend to promise results – 'High test scores or your money back'.

A good many of these ventures will surely fail. Still, they will be launched in large numbers. As knowledge becomes the resource of post-capitalist society, the social position of the 'producer' and 'distributive channel' of knowledge, that is, of the school, and its monopoly position are both bound to be challenged. And some of the competitors are bound to succeed.

What will be taught and learned; how it will be taught and learned; the customers of schooling and school; and the position of the school in society – they all will thus change greatly during the next decades. Indeed, no other institution faces challenges as radical as those that will transform schooling and school.

But the greatest change – and the one we are least prepared for – is that the school will have to commit itself to results. It will have to establish its 'bottom line', that is, the performance for which it should be held responsible, and for which it is being paid. *The school will become accountable.*

12

The Educated Person

This book deals with the environment in which man lives, works and learns. It does not deal with the person. But in the knowledge society into which we are moving, the person is central. Knowledge is not impersonal like money. Knowledge does not reside in a book, a data bank, a software program. They contain only information. Knowledge is always embodied in a person, taught and learned by a person, used or misused by a person. The shift to the knowledge society therefore puts the person in the centre. In doing so it raises new challenges, new issues, new and quite unprecedented questions regarding the knowledge society's representative, the *Educated Person*.

In all earlier societies the Educated Person was ornament. He or she were *Kultur* – the German term which, in its mixture of awe and derision, is untranslatable into English (even 'highbrow' does not come close). But in the knowledge society the Educated Person is society's emblem; society's symbol; society's standard bearer. The Educated Person is the social 'archetype' – to use the sociologist's term. He or she defines society's performance capacity. But he or she also embodies society's values, beliefs, commitments. If the feudal knight *was* society in the early Middle Ages; and if the 'burgeois' *was* society in Capitalism; the Educated Person *will be* society in the post-capitalist society in which knowledge has become the central resource.

This must change the very meaning of Educated Person. It must change what it means to be educated. It will thus predictably make the definition of Educated Person a crucial issue. With knowledge becoming the key resource, the Educated Person faces new demands, new challenges, new responsibilities. *He and she now matter*.

For the last 10 or 15 years a vigorous – and often shrill – debate has been raging in American academia over the Educated Person. Should there be one? Could there be one? And what should be considered 'education' altogether?

A motley crew of post-Marxists, radical feminists and other 'antis' argues that there can be no such thing as an Educated Person – the position of those new Nihilists, the 'Deconstructionsts'. Others in this group assert that there can be only Educated Person*s*, with each sex, each ethnic group, each race, each 'minority', requiring its own separate culture and a separate – indeed an isolationist – Educated Person. Since these people are mainly concerned with the 'humanities' there are few echoes as yet of Hitler's 'Aryan Physics', Stalin's 'Marxist Genetics' or Mao's 'Communist Psychology'. But the arguments of these anti-traditionalists recall those of the totalitarians. And their target is the same: the universalism that is at the very core of the concept of an Educated Person whatever it may be called, i.e. 'Educated Person' as in the West or *bunjin* as in China and Japan.

The opposing camp – it might be called the 'Humanists' – also scorns the present system, but because it fails to produce a universal Educated Person. The Humanist critics demand a return to the nineteenth century, to the 'Liberal Arts', the 'Classics', the German *Gebildete Mensch*. They do not, so far, repeat the assertion made by Robert Hutchins and Mortimer Adler 50 years ago at the University of Chicago that 'knowledge' in its entirety consists of a few 'great books'. But they are in direct line of descent from the Hutchins-Adler 'Return to Pre-Modernity'.

Both sides, alas, are wrong. The knowledge society *must* have at its core the concept of the Educated Person. It will have to be a universal concept, precisely because the knowledge society is a society of knowledges, and because it is global – in its money, its economics, its careers, its technology, its central issues, and, above all, in its information. Post-capitalist society requires a unifying force. It requires a leadership group which can focus local, particular, separate traditions onto a common and shared commitment to values, onto a common concept of excellence, and onto mutual respect.

The post-capitalist society, the knowledge society, thus needs exactly the opposite of what Deconstructionsts, Radical Feminists or Anti-Westerners propose. It needs the very thing they totally reject: a universal Educated Person.

Yet the knowledge society needs a different Educated Person from the ideal for which the Humanists fight. They rightly stress the folly of their opponents' demand for a repudiation of the Great Tradition and of the wisdom, beauty, knowledge, that are the heritage of mankind. But to have a bridge to the past is not enough. And that is all the Humanists offer. The Educated Person needs to be able to bring his or her knowledge to bear on the present, if not to mould the future. There is no provision for such ability in the proposals of the Humanists, indeed no concern for it. But without it the Great Tradition is dusty antiquarianism.

In his 1943 novel *Das Glasperlenspiel* (*The Glass Bead Game*: English translation under the title *Magister Ludi*, 1949) the Swiss-German Nobel Prize winner Hermann Hesse (1877–1962) anticipated the world the Humanists want – and its failure. The book depicts a brotherhood of intellectuals, artists and humanists who live a life of splendid isolation, dedicated to the Great Tradition, its wisdom and its beauty. But the book's hero, the most accomplished Master of the Brotherhood, decides, in the end, to return to polluted, crass, vulgar, turbulent, strife-torn, money-grubbing reality – for his values are only fool's gold unless they have relevance to the world.

What Hesse more than 50 years ago foresaw is now happening. 'Liberal Education' and *Allgemeine Bildung* are in crisis today because they have become a *Glasperlenspiel* which the brightest desert for crass, vulgar, money-grubbing reality. The ablest students enjoy the Liberal Arts. They enjoy them fully as much as did their great-grandparents who graduated before World War I. For that earlier generation 'Liberal Arts' and *Allgemeine Bildung* remained meaningful throughout their lives. It defined their identity. It still remained meaningful for many members of my generation which graduated before World War II – even though we immediately forgot our Latin and Greek. But today's students all say a few years after they have graduated: 'What I have learned so eagerly has no meaning; it has no relevance to anything I do, am interested in, want to become.' For their children they still want the Liberals Arts College, Princeton or Carleton, Oxbridge, Tokyo University, the *Lycée*, the *Gymnasium* – though mainly for social status and access to good jobs. But in their own lives they repudiate 'Liberal Education' and *Allgemeine Bildung*. They repudiate the Educated Person of the Humanists. The Liberal Education does not enable them to understand reality, let alone to master it.

Both sides in the present debate are largely irrelevant. Post-capitalist society needs an Educated Person – more than any earlier society. Access to the great heritage of the past will have to be an essential element. In fact 'past' will have to embrace a good deal more than the Humanists fight for. Theirs is still mainly 'Western civilization' and 'Judaeo-Christian tradition'. It is still nineteenth century. The Educated Person we need will have to be able to appreciate other great cultures and traditions: the great heritage of Chinese, Japanese, Korean paintings and ceramics; the philosophers and the great religions of the Orient; and Islam, both as a religion and as a culture. The Educated Person also will have to be far less exclusively 'bookish' than the Liberal Education of the Humanists. He or she will need trained perception fully as much as analysis.

The Western tradition will still have to be at the core, if only to enable the Educated Person to come to grips with the present, let alone with the future. The future may be 'post-Western'. It may be 'anti-Western'. It cannot be 'non-Western'. Its material civilization and its knowledges rest on Western foundations: science; tools and technology; production; economics; money, finance and banking. None of these can work unless grounded in both understanding and acceptance of Western ideas and of the Western tradition altogether.

The early nineteenth-century West African who carved the wooden masks which the developed countries so eagerly collect now knew nothing of the West and owed little to it. His descendant in West Africa who carves wooden masks today – and some are extraordinarily powerful – still lives in a mud hut in the tribal village. His country may not even be 'underdeveloped' yet. Still, he has a radio, a TV set and a motorbike. He uses new tools, all of them products of Western technology. He carves for an art dealer in Paris or New York. His aesthetics owe as much to the German Expressionists and to Picasso as they owe to his own West African ancestor.

The most profoundly 'anti-Western' movement today is not Fundamentalist Islam. It is the revolt of the 'Shining Path' in Peru – the desperate attempt of the descendants of the Incas to make undone the Spanish Conquests to go back to the Indians' ancient tongues of Quechua and Aymara, and to drive the hated Europeans and their culture back into the ocean. Shining Path finances itself by growing coca for the drug addicts of New York and Los Angeles. Its favourite weapon is not the Incas' sling shot. It is the car bomb.

Tomorrow's Educated Persons will have to be prepared for living in a global world. It will be a 'Westernized' world. But the Educated Persons will also live in an increasingly tribalized world. They must be able to be 'citizens of the world' – in their vision, their horizon, their information. But they will also have to draw nourishment from their local roots and, in turn, enrich and nourish their own local culture.

Post-capitalist society is both a Knowledge Society and a Society of Organizations, each dependent on the other and yet different in its concepts, views, values. Most, if not all, Educated Persons will (as said earlier in this book) practise their knowledge as members of an organization. The Educated Person will therefore have to be prepared to live and work simultaneously in two cultures, that of the 'intellectual' who focuses on words and ideas, and that of the 'manager' who focuses on people and work.

Intellectuals need the organization as a tool; it enables them to practise their *téchne*, their specialized knowledge. Managers see knowledge as a means to the end of organizational performance. Both are right. They are opposites; but they relate to each other as *poles* rather than as contradictions. They need each other. The research scientist needs the research manager and the research manager needs the research scientist. If one overbalances the other there is only non-performance and all-round frustration. The intellectual's world, unless counterbalanced by the manager, becomes one in which everybody 'does his own thing' but nobody does anything. The manager's world, unless counterbalanced by the intellectual, becomes bureaucracy and the stultifying greyness of the 'organization man'. But if the two balance each other there can be creativity and order, fulfillment and mission.

A good many people in the post-capitalist society will actually live and work in these two cultures at the same time. And many more could – and should – be exposed to working experience in both cultures, by rotation early in their career, from a specialist's job to a managerial one, for instance, by rotating the young computer technician into being project manager and team leader, or by asking the young college professor to work part-time for two years in university administration. And again, working as 'unpaid staff' in an agency of the social sector will give the individual the perspective, the balance to see, know, respect both worlds, that of the intellectual and that of the manager.

And all Educated Persons in the post-capitalist society will have to be prepared to *understand* both cultures.

For the nineteenth-century Educated Person *téchnes* were not knowledge. They were already taught in the university. They had become 'disciplines'. Their practitioners were 'professionals', rather than 'tradesmen' or 'artisans'. But they were not part of the Liberal Arts or of the *Allgemeine Bildung* and thus not part of knowledge.

There long had been university degrees in *téchnes*: in Europe both the law degree and the medical degree go back to the thirteenth century. And on the European continent and in America – though not in England – the new engineering degree (first awarded in Napoleon's France a year or two before 1800) soon became socially accepted. Most people who were considered 'educated' made their living practising a *téchne* – as lawyers, physicians, engineers, geologists, and increasingly in business (in fact only in England was there esteem for the 'gentleman' without occupation). But their job or their profession was a 'living', and not their 'life'.

Outside of their offices, the *téchne* practitioners did not talk about their work or even about their disciplines. It was 'shop talk'. The Germans sneered at it as *Fachsimpeln*. It was even more derided in France. Anyone who indulged in it was considered both a boor and a bore and promptly taken off the invitation lists of 'polite society'.

But now that the *téchnes* have become knowledges they have to be integrated into knowledge. The *téchnes* have to become part of what it is to be an Educated Person. That the liberal arts they enjoyed so much in their college years do not do that, cannot do that – in fact refuse even to try – is the reason why today's students repudiate them a few years later. They feel let down, indeed, betrayed. They have good reason to feel that way. Liberal Arts and *Allgemeine Bildung* which do not integrate the knowledges into a 'universe of knowledge' are neither 'liberal' nor *Bildung*. They fall down on their first task: to create mutual understanding – that 'universe of discourse' without which there can be no civilization. Instead of uniting, such liberal arts fragment.

We neither need nor will get 'polymaths' who are at home in many knowledges. We will probably become even more specialized. But what we do need – and what will define the Educated Person in the Knowledge Society – is ability to *understand* the knowledges. What is each about? What is it trying to do? What are its central concerns? What are its central theories? What major new insights has it produced? What are its important areas of ignorance, its problems, its challenges?

Without such understanding the knowledges themselves will become sterile, will indeed cease to be 'knowledges'. They will become intellectual arrogant and unproductive. For the major new insights in every one of the specialized knowledges are coming out of another, separate, specialty, that is, out of another one of the knowledges.

Both economics and meteorology are being transformed at present by the new mathematics of Chaos Theory. Geology is being profoundly changed by the physics of matter; archaeology by the genetics of DNA typing; history by psychological, statistical and technological analyses and techniques. An American, James M. Buchanan (born 1919), received the 1986 Nobel Prize in Economics for applying recent economic theory to the political process and thereby standing on their head the assumptions and theories on which political scientists had based their work for over a century.

To make knowledges into knowledge requires that the holders of the knowledges, the specialists, take responsibility for making *understood* both themselves and their knowledge area.

The 'media' – whether magazines, movies, television – have a crucial role to play. But they cannot do the job by themselves. Nor can any other kind of popularization. The knowledges must be understood as what they are: serious, rigorous, demanding. This requires that the leaders in each of the knowledges – beginning with the leading scholars in each field – take responsibility for making their own knowledge understood and are willing to do the hard work this requires.

There is no 'Queen of the Knowledges' in the knowledge society. All knowledges are equally valuable, all knowledges, in the words of the great medieval saint and philosopher, St Bonaventura, equally lead to the truth. But to make them paths to truth, paths to knowledge, has to be the responsibility of the men and women of the knowledges. Collectively they hold knowledge in trust.

Capitalism had been dominant for over a century when Karl Marx in *Das Kapital* (first volume published in 1867) identified it as a distinct social order. The term 'Capitalism' was not coined until 30 years later, well after Marx's death. It would therefore not only be presumptuous in the extreme to attempt to write *The Knowledge* today; it would be ludicrously premature. All that can be attempted – all this book attempts – is to describe society and polity as we begin the transition from the Age of Capitalism (which, of course, was also the Age of Socialism).

But we can hope that a hundred years hence a book of this kind, if not a book entitled *Knowledge*, can and will be written. That would mean that we have successfully weathered the transition upon which we have embarked. It would be as foolish to predict the Knowledge Society as it would have been foolish to predict in 1776 – the year of the American Revolution, of Adam Smith's *Wealth of Nations*, and of James Watt's steam engine – the society of which Marx wrote a hundred years later – and as it was foolish of Marx to predict in mid-Victorian Capitalism – and with 'scientific infallibility' – the post-capitalist society in which we now live.

But one thing is predictable: the greatest change will be the change in knowledge; in its form and content; in its meaning; in its responsibility; and in what it means to be an Educated Person.

Index